ALICE

ROBERTA KELLS DORR

BROADMAN PRESS
Nashville, Tennessee

ISBN: 0-8054-5080-7
Dewey Decimal Classification: 266.53
Subject Headings: MISSIONS// GAZA//
DORR, ROBERTA KELLS
Library of Congress Catalog Number: 88-35602

Printed in the United States of America

Library of Congress Cataloging-in-Publication Data

Dorr, Roberta Kells.
   Alice / Roberta Kells Dorr.
     p.   cm.
   ISBN 0-8054-5080-7
   1. Alice.   2. Baptists—Gaza Strip—Biography.   3. Missions—Gaza
Strip.   4. Dorr, Roberta Kells.   I. Title.
BX6495.A43D67   1989
266'.6132'0924—dc19
[B]   88-35602
                                             CIP

Contents

CHAPTER
1

I shall never forget that day in London, walking down Minories Street toward Tower Bridge and hearing the menacing roar of an angry crowd. As we turned the corner on Eastcheap the noise grew louder, and we could see a young man dressed in a faded blue suit standing on a low wall clutching a red book. He was trying to talk to a large crowd of rough-looking men who were shouting and shaking their fists at him.

Our children had never seen anyone talking on the street, and they begged to be allowed to go closer. We hesitated. There were no other women or children in the group, and the men looked tough and hostile. We edged closer, hoping to hear what was being said that had so upset these men. Philip, our sixteen-year-old, and his younger brother Paul edged into the center of the group and worked their way down to the front where they could see what was going on. Debby gave me a fleeting look as if to ask permission and then ran to join her older brothers, while Putts grabbed my hand and Jimmy asked his father to hold him so he could see over the shifting heads of the mob.

It was getting late. The Tower would soon be closed to tourists, but the children were right in the midst of the angry group of men and there was no choice but to stay. The young man was not preaching. He seemed to be trying to reason quietly with these men, but it was obvious on closer scrutiny that the red book he held was a Bible. Our curiosity mounted and we moved closer. His voice was clear and now came to us quite distinctly. We could tell he was telling them that God loved them and wanted to help them.

I was astonished. This quiet young man and his message of God's love was what this mob of angry men had taken issue with and were objecting to.

"You're a fool! You're a fool," they shouted, trying to drown out his words.

"Es a blinkin' fool bigger than most ah've seen." The red-faced, tousled-haired bully pulled away from the crowd and tried to stand right in front of the young man to silence him. The rest of the men joked and laughed, nudging each other.

"Hey, you," a big burly man said. He was weaving on his feet from too many mugs of beer, and as he pushed his way to the front he shook his fist in the young man's face. "Tell me one miracle, just one miracle that this Jesus has done, and I'll listen to you. He ain't never done nothin' for me."

He turned to the men, "Has this Jesus ever done anythin' for any of you?"

The men were now bunched together in a tight, angry knot, and they moved forward as they began to chant, "No! No! No! He ain't never done nothin' for us."

The young man tried to speak but their shouting drowned him out. "Show us. Just show us somethin E's done? Show us one miracle E's ever done."

Our children pushed their way back through the jeering men with Debby reaching me first. "Mother," she shouted over the raucous laughter and stomping feet. "Tell them about Alice."

The boys tugged at David's coat, "Dad, tell them about Alice."

By this time the young man had jumped down from the wall and the surly group of men moved away. David and I looked at each other helplessly. We would have loved to tell them about Alice and all that God had done for us, but it was too late. We were still in a jet-lag daze from our recent flight into London on our way home from the Middle East. We had just come from the Gaza Strip where my husband was a surgeon working with the Palestinian refugees. We were exhausted and now a bit shocked that in Christian England there could be such a large group of men that had never felt God at work in their lives nor had ever seen a miracle. We had been through the furnace of sickness, loneliness, death, and war, but we had seen miracles and had felt God's love in our lives. As we turned away and walked toward the ticket gate in front of the Tower, we were mostly frustrated and disappointed in ourselves that we had stood by almost paralyzed, saying nothing while that young man had faced the mob alone. It seemed that at least we could have said something, and yet, what? Where could we begin telling what God had done for us?

Perhaps Debby was right. Maybe we couldn't tell it all, but if we could just tell them about Alice. Even to tell about Alice would not be easy. One would have to hear the whole story from the beginning.

I took the ticket and waited while David and the children went hurrying toward the gate. I wanted to see what had happened to the young man. He was gone, but some of the men were still there, laughing and waving their arms as though making fun of him. *I guess I really should write the story of Alice,* I thought to myself. Now, at last, here is that story.

CHAPTER

2

I have often tried to remember when I first noticed Alice. She had been there all along, observing me just as she observed everyone else. She would have noticed whether I smiled or turned away, put out my hand or hurried on, shared my hymnbook or pondered alone over the new script and difficult Arabic words. She was never critical and would have noticed only out of curiosity that I did not cover my head with a scarf as was the custom for Arab Christian women in church, put on too much makeup for these conservative people, and constantly wore shoes with heels that were unsuited to the dirt paths and sandy soil. *She will learn, but it takes time,* Alice would have concluded.

She would have observed with concern that we were awkward at pronouncing the new-sounding names, could not distinguish one coin from another, and did not seem to realize that many of the Arabic words being taught our children by the nurses, cleaners, and gardners at the hospital were swear words. Nothing would have escaped her interest.

Within a month she would have known that I sometimes played tennis with my husband and found it difficult to play the organ because in Arabic the notes were printed "backwards." She would have seen when I squirmed impatiently during the long Sunday service in Arabic and would have concluded with some surprise that I could not understand one word of what was being said.

During this same time I had not noticed Alice, and when I finally did learn her name, I knew very little about her. I knew that she taught school, was unmarried, and had been the first person to be baptized in our baptistry and to become a member of our church. I knew nothing more and, worse, assumed there was very little more to learn.

It was quite by chance that I ever came to really know Alice. I can vividly remember the time, place, and even the atmosphere on that late spring afternoon when Alice stopped by our house dressed in a very expensive red lace dress. I had never before noticed what Alice wore. Her clothes were usually nondescript and clean but scarcely memorable.

I had been busy teaching one of our children the multiplication tables, and the rest were having recess when Alice arrived. "Your dress is pretty enough to wear to a wedding," I casually remarked, as I led her to the more intimate sitting room that opened off the front entryway.

"You like it?" Alice asked. "I had it made especially for the occasion. It isn't a wedding." Her eyes sparkled and invited me to ask more questions.

"If it isn't a wedding, it must be an engagement."

"You are right," she said, refusing the cup of tea I offered to bring.

"I don't have time for tea today. I must hurry." I could see that she wanted to tell me about it and yet, for some reason, she was silent.

"Is it someone I know?" I asked, hopefully.

"No, you don't know her but there is a story, an interesting story. They want me to be in the picture they are having taken, because, in a way, I'm responsible for this engagement." Alice was about thirty and had avoided marriage rather consistently, though the subject had been a matter of concern to her family for years. Now she had whetted my curiosity. I knew there must be something very unusual about this engagement, but in spite of all my coaxing she would not tell me anything more.

"We will see," she said, smiling happily. "Maybe I will tell you tomorrow." I stood at the door and watched her walk down the steps and out to the large green gate that led from the hospital compound directly onto the main street of Gaza. There were always groups of men sitting on some of the low wooden stools in the shade of the gate house. Old Able Obed, the gateman, got up slowly and opened the small postern gate to let her pass. There was a blur of red suspended for a moment against the dull green of the gate, and then she was gone.

I closed the screen door and went back into our house and up the long stairway to the schoolroom. The desks were all moved out of place, and I had the feeling that Paul had barely settled back into his seat. I heard giggles and shuffling of feet out on the veranda. "All right," I called to the unseen gigglers, "Your recess is over. It's back to work for all of you." Kay and Jo Young with Debby burst through the door and hurried to their seats, carefully concealing a baby kitten under the lid of one of the desks. "No cats," I said, ushering the offender out and bringing Mark Young and Philip back into the classroom.

I stood for a moment and watched them push their desks back into place, then glanced out onto the veranda where Putts was riding a small tricycle back and forth with appropriate noises as though he were driving a donkey cart. Im Halad squatted near the railing, her faded blue dress pulled taut over her thin knees, her mantle hanging loose down to her bare feet. She was watching Jimmy play and would keep the boys quiet while I taught the others. As we picked up the reading books and I flipped through the pages to the lesson for that day, I thought briefly of Alice: *Perhaps when she comes to the chapel on Sunday she will tell me all about the mysterious engagement.*

Sundays were always the same. The bell summoned the nurses and students to their shifts at the hospital and the doctors to "make rounds." For most of the city it was just another work day, and only at the Greek Orthodox church and the Baptist chapel was any service held. Alice taught school and was able to come to the chapel only between classes.

I waited for her outside the chapel near one of the free-standing pillars. These pillars were unique to the hospital. I was told they had been found years ago on the beach by one of the British doctors and brought here. Now they served only to mark the place where people coming early to church or the clinic waited to meet their friends.

Alice was late. The music from the old pump organ was announcing the first hymn when I saw her come hurrying through the gate and up the path. I plied her with questions but she simply smiled and shook her head. "There is no time now." she said. "Wait, be patient." She held up her hand, fingers closed against the thumb in the typical Arabic gesture meaning, "be patient, wait." Her eyes again twinkled with delight, and I realized that what she had to tell me was too special to be conveyed casually while walking the few steps to the chapel.

When the service was over she had to hurry back to school and I walked with her to the gate. "All right," I said quickly, trying to be heard above the honking horns and the music from a coffeehouse across the street, "All right, you must come on Friday, your day off." She turned once to wave and then I watched as she squeezed into the backseat of a waiting taxi.

Friday arrived with the early morning call to prayer coming first from the old mosque in the middle of the city and then rising in a strange, discordant mingling with the call from other mosques, some nearer and some more distant. There would be one more half hour to sleep before the bell clanged at the hospital, waking the doctors and nurses for chapel and another day of work.

Long before the chapel bell rang, David had been up and dressed and off to the hospital to make rounds. Mahmoud had coffee steaming on the small primus in the kitchen and Im Halad was mopping the floor. I could hear the swishing sound of the coarse cloth as she bent and circled it over the tile floor that had again become coated with dust since the previous morning. I could hear her dousing the cloth up and down in the mop pail, the twisting, splashing noise of the cloth being squeezed, and then the sickening smell of kerosene that came under the door and was the final signal that it was time to get up. *I wish there was something else other than kerosene to cut dust and leave the tiles bright*, I thought as I bounded out of bed and dressed, remembering only briefly that it was Friday, visiting day at the hospital and in our homes. I would try to have school anyway. *At least until recess*, I determined.

Alice came as she had promised. She had made *cousa mashi* (stuffed zucchini) which she left in the kitchen, explaining to Mahmoud how to warm it so it wouldn't get overcooked. "You have time?" she asked, and I nodded, scooping up the tea tray with its cups and steaming pot of Gaza tea.

"We will sit in here where we won't be interrupted," I said, pushing open the door and setting the tea tray down before the sofa. I opened the drapes made of heavy satin cotton from Cairo and opened a window to let in some fresh air. This parlor was small and private and had probably been used in this same way by the British doctors who built this huge house when they had first come to Gaza in the early 1890s. No child dared play in this room, as it contained the only furniture we had brought from home. In a dim light this small parlor could look quite elegant.

Alice sat in the straight-backed chair, and I settled down on the sofa. She played hostess, serving my cup of tea and remembering that I drank it plain with no cream or sugar. She didn't want the cookies, and her own cup was poured and getting cold. "Don't mind," she said, "about the tea. I've come to tell you about something very wonderful. I don't tell everyone because they won't believe. I've tried. But you must listen and then come with me and you will see for yourself that it is true."

"Do you remember last Christmas?" she asked. "It was in the early evening after the Christmas program. I was waiting for the singspiration time, and you and Mrs. Young were busy fixing dinner for all of those UNEF soldiers, when I saw a girl sitting on a bench by herself over under the marmalade tree. She was crying and didn't notice me until I sat down beside her. She turned her back and tried to hide her tears, and I asked her why she was crying." Alice looked at me to see if I understood and then hurried on.

"Her name was Nadia, and she was in despair because she had not passed her exams and could not teach. She pictured herself sitting at home sewing and cooking and getting old like so many of the women she knew. She is Christian," Alice explained. "The Christians and Moslems of Gaza have never intermarried."

Since the earliest days of the church there had been Christians in Gaza, and even after the Moslem conquest of this area there were Christians who refused to give up their faith. There are now about two thousand of these Christians living in Gaza, most of them are educated teachers, pharmacists, and goldsmiths, but all of them have clung to their identity as Christians. "They have some problems," Alice said. "One of them is that there are just not enough Christian young men to go around. If a girl does not have a cousin to marry and does not come from rich family, she will either have to teach or remain at home. I could see that since Nadia had not passed her exam to teach and there was no young man for her to marry, the future did look very black to her."

"But," I interrupted, "You were going to an engagement?"

"Wait, wait," Alice laughed at my impatience, holding up her hand in the familiar gesture of the pinched fingers. "There is an engagement, but you have to hear it as it happened or you will miss the miracle that God performed for Nadia.

"That day when I saw her sitting on the bench crying," Alice continued, "I asked her if she believed in God's power to change hopeless situations. She said she did, and I suggested that we go back to the church and talk to God about her problem.

"We went back, and she prayed first with tears and then, in real despair, she poured out her whole heart before God. I prayed next, and when I had finished I knew the answer. 'Within three months a young man will come from Egypt,' I said, 'He is a good young man. He is rich and he will ask you to marry him. You will be happy with him. So do not be afraid, but trust that God will do as He has said.' "

"Alice," I broke into her story, "You told her a young man would come from Egypt and would ask to marry her? Did you know this young man?"

"No, of course not," Alice said, as though this were already obvious.

"Then how could you tell this girl a young man would come from Egypt and ask to marry her?" Alice paused and looked puzzled for a moment as she saw my own bewilderment.

"You don't understand," she began patiently, "as we prayed God answered our prayers and I knew it would be so."

"You knew it would be so?" I was leaning forward trying to understand.

She smiled patiently, "It happens to me often but I usually don't mention it because no one believes."

I hurried to reassure her, "It isn't that I don't believe, but just that I have never in my life heard such a thing."

"Let me finish the story, and then you will believe," she assured me. "The three months passed, and of course I did not see the girl again until the family called me for her engagement."

"Then someone did come and ask to marry her?" I asked, hardly daring to move my eyes from Alice's face lest I miss some hint of the meaning of what I had heard.

"Of course," she said, almost impatient at my questioning.

"From Egypt?" I whispered.

"From Egypt." She said.

"He was rich?" I asked, as though seeking to find some little portion of the prediction that had not come true, in order to bolster my view of how things usually seemed to happen even in the realm of answered prayer.

"He was so rich. . . ." Alice stopped suddenly. The happy light died from her eyes and she seemed to draw back into some quiet reserve. I saw that she was not going to tell me more and I was immediately sorry I had questioned her so sternly and so abruptly. "You don't believe," she said sadly.

"It isn't that I don't believe," I said, struggling to find words to express my hesitancy and what I would have proudly called at some other time my analytical mind. "You have to understand, Alice," I countered in my own defense, "I believe God answers prayer, but in quite a normal fashion and without the foreknowledge and the details you describe. . . . This is too much for me. Someone from Egypt, in three months, came and asked this girl he had never seen before to marry him and, more than that, he is rich just as you told her?" I was incredulous.

It was evident that Alice was puzzled that I seemed to have such a mental barrier to belief. No matter how much I trusted Alice and how much I would like to believe that God could do something that amazing, I found it difficult. *There had to be some missing piece to the story,* I reasoned. Perhaps Alice thought this was how it happened, or perhaps she herself was so trusting she would believe anything without checking out the facts.

We sat in silence only faintly conscious of the outdoor noises coming in through the open window and the laughter of children running down the stairs. Finally Alice stood up. "You don't believe," she said sadly, "but if you came and saw the girl and let her tell the story herself perhaps then you could believe that what I've told you really happened."

I was immediately excited. "Oh, Alice, that would be wonderful. If I could go and see her and hear it from her lips perhaps. . . ."

"Tomorrow I will come and take you to her," Alice said as she moved toward the door. "It will have to be in the afternoon when school is out."

I hurried after her, "Will it be imposing on them if I come tomorrow, so soon?"

Alice turned, and I could see that she was not angry with me, but the bright happy light was gone from her eyes. "No, they love to tell anyone who will listen. They will show you the pictures. You will see, they insisted on taking one of me, too."

"In the red dress?" I asked.

"In the red dress," she said smiling, as she closed the screen and hurried down the steps, leaving me to ponder all that had happened and to wonder what I would learn when I visited the family the next day.

CHAPTER

3

It was already crisp and cool with sudden showers of rain, but when Alice came to get me the sky was clearing and there was the strange stillness that always followed a shower. The palm trees and hedges were dripping and the four-o'clocks had not yet closed for the night. The bright yellow calendulas and nasturtiums edged the inner wall of the compound and looked like pieces of sunshine trapped beside our path.

When we walked through the small postern door within the larger gate, we stepped out into another world. The street was now rutted and pooled. The taxis carrying passengers honked and spattered mud while carts pulled by donkeys wove in and out as they tried to avoid the puddles. Suddenly a taxi driver beside us honked his horn and leaned out of the window to shout abuse at an old man for walking in front of his car. Without taking advantage of the situation, Alice banged on the opposite window until the driver rolled it down impatiently.

"To Ramal?" she asked. He must have nodded, because she opened the door and we crowded in with the other passengers. She handed him the fare while I searched in my purse and counted out the money. She wouldn't take it. We argued all the way down toward the beach and the Ramal quarter of Gaza.

One by one the passengers got out and Alice leaned forward and spoke quietly to the driver. He objected with stubborn determination, and she continued to talk quietly but persistently. She handed him something and the dialogue ended. He turned off the main road and splashed recklessly through the rutted, mud-filled lane that was wedged between the high walls of villas that lined either side of the street.

"I asked him to drive us to the door," Alice explained. "He's very obstinate. I told him you couldn't walk far in the mud with those high heels."

"Oh Alice, I'm so sorry," I said, realizing that I had caused her extra trouble because I was not used to wearing shoes for walking.

"Don't worry," she smiled, "we want to get there as soon as possible. I only used your shoes as an excuse."

Within minutes we were out of the taxi and standing on the small portion of tile outside a large, wrought-iron gate. Alice rang the bell. While we waited, I had time to study the street and the house in front of us. The wall was too high to look over. Only at the gate was it possible to peek through the carved grillwork and see the fine house standing at the end of the walkway lined with orange and lemon trees. This was a family of means we were visiting, and I was strangely surprised.

"*Ahlan, Ahlan,*" the voice was warm and welcoming. There was the sound of a heavy bolt being pulled back and a key turning before the iron gate swung open to reveal the woman who had welcomed us. She was small and dark haired with a shawl around her shoulders to keep out the cold. She shook my hand and reached to embrace Alice warmly. She was obviously excited to see Alice, and the two talked in Arabic while I followed them to the wide veranda and through the open front door into a parlor.

Here Nadia's mother led me to the seat of honor, a cushioned wicker loveseat, and motioned for Alice to sit in the chair beside me. I barely had time to glance around the room. There were chairs in the usual circle and a wicker table prepared for tea. With shy giggles and murmured welcomes, the rest of the girls and women of the family came in to greet me. There were the old grandmother, one or two younger women, children still dressed in their school uniforms, and, last of all, a beautiful young girl who introduced herself as Nadia.

Fortunately, Nadia spoke English, but she was so shy that at first she simply drank the tea that was served us while I asked unimportant questions about the family in general, using almost all of my new Arabic vocabulary. The family enjoyed hearing me struggle to say the unfamiliar words and gradually we felt more comfortable with each other.

Alice said nothing. She neither tried to help me out with my Arabic sentences nor did she answer for the family when I found it hard to understand what they were saying. Gradually, Nadia began to interpret into English those words I couldn't understand.

By the time the tea things were carried away, Nadia was relaxed and confident enough to speak to me without hesitation. "Nadia, tell Mrs. Dorr about your engagement," Alice urged.

Nadia blushed, "Oh, it's so exciting! I don't know where to begin."

"Here, show her the pictures." The mother had brought in a large photo album and, as they both flipped over the pages looking for the best pictures, I caught glimpses of bright colors, many flowers, and became more and more curious to see what the "young man" from Egypt would look like. Finally, they turned back to the first page and handed me the book. "You see, there is Yousef," Nadia said, blushing while the little girls all laughed at her shyness.

I saw an enlarged, color photo of a dark-haired young man with large, friendly, brown eyes. "He's very handsome," I said. "He reminds me of someone I have seen someplace, only he is younger."

"Omar Sharif," one of the young girls said, and everyone laughed again as I immediately agreed that he really did look like a younger version of the famous Egyptian movie star.

"How did you meet a young man from Egypt?" I asked Nadia.

Instantly everyone began to talk at once, trying to outtalk each other in telling the story. The little girls crowded around and the older women leaned forward eagerly, each wanting to be heard above the others. Finally, Alice stood up and spoke quickly in Arabic, leading the little girls back to their seats and motioning to me. "She will have to hear the story from Nadia. She doesn't understand the language well enough yet for all of you to talk in

Arabic." I could make out that much of what was being said, and I noticed that all of them nodded their agreement as Nadia took a deep breath, pushed back the long hair from her face, and leaned toward me, ready to tell her story.

"Yousef," she said, "was sent here to buy a car from Gaza. You know they import very few new cars in Egypt, and his family is wealthy and wanted a new car."

She paused and I silently marveled: "He is Egyptian, very handsome, and now I find he is rich." I was even more curious to hear how Nadia had met him and how they had become engaged so fast.

"How did you meet him?" I said, wanting to skip all the incidentals and get to the point that interested me most.

"Oh, that was very strange," Nadia said. "I was walking home from school with some of my friends. We were in our uniforms and, being a Christian girl, I didn't have my face covered. Yousef was on the other side of the street, walking with the friend at whose house he was staying. He asked the friend, 'Do you know the girl walking in the center of those girls across the strees?'

"Yousef's friend said he knew my family but, of course, did not know me."

"Could you introduce me to her family?" Yousef asked his friend.

"Why do you want to meet her family?" the friend asked.

"Because that is the girl I want to marry," Yousef said.

I was so astonished I stopped Nadia. "How did Yousef know he wanted to marry you without even meeting you?"

"That's not so strange when you understand that at home he was expected to marry his cousin. It is the custom in Egypt among the Christians. When he came to Gaza and saw me he decided he wanted to marry someone he chose rather than someone his parents chose. He saw me and he chose me, even though it is more expensive for an Egyptian to marry a Gaza girl. In Egypt the girl buys much of the furniture, but in Gaza the young man has to buy everything: clothes, jewelry, and furniture for their home."

"Did he come then to meet your family?" I asked, eager to hear all the story. I was aware that I had heard no mention of Alice and her predictions yet.

She turned over some pages in the book. "He came, and my parents told him he must do everything properly and according to our custom, and he agreed to everything."

"Did you see each other when he came to your home?" I asked.

"Yes, we spoke to each other, and we knew that we loved each other right away. Of course, we were never alone, but we knew how we felt about each other. It was really a miracle. If it hadn't been for Alice it would never have happened." She turned through the pages to the engagement pictures, and I saw the picture of the two young people seated together with Alice in the red lace dress standing beside them smiling as I had seen her smile that day when she stopped at my door.

I glanced at Nadia and saw that she was looking at Alice with a fond smile. "You see, Alice told me all of this would happen when she found me crying near the Ingleese church at Christmastime. I came home and told my family, and they all laughed and teased me about it. I was the only one who believed it would happen. When Yousef did come and they saw that he was an Egyptian and rich, my mother and father were terribly surprised. But they didn't object because they knew that what Alice had told me had been from God and that she had also told me that we would be happy together."

I looked at Alice and saw how amused she was at my surprise to find the story from Nadia was just as she had told it to me. I still had one more question for Nadia. "If Alice had not told you that all this would happen in just this way, would your parents have allowed you to marry this young man they knew nothing about?"

Nadia's mother wanted to know what I had asked and Nadia repeated the question to her in Arabic. The mother shook her head firmly, and I could tell that she was saying that it would have been impossible for them to give their daughter to an unknown Egyptian, no matter how rich and how many gifts he brought, if they had not known it was God's will.

"No, you see, that is part of the miracle," Nadia explained. "Alice had said that within three months an Egyptian would come who was handsome and rich, and there he was. They could not deny it had all come true in such an amazing way that only God could have done it. That is why we wanted Alice in the picture. It was a miracle, and we always want to remember how it all came about."

I looked at the picture again and saw the tall, handsome, young man sitting very stiffly in the decorated chair with Nadia sitting beside him, almost unrecognizable in her carefully made-up face, expertly coiffured hair, and elegant dress, a gift from Egypt brought to her by the groom. The only face that was natural and familiar in the picture was Alice's. The red lace dress seemed a bit foreign, but the face was radiant with joy.

I flashed Alice an apologetic glance. I still did not understand it any more than I had when I first heard the story. However, now I knew it was just as Alice had told me, but I wanted to put it in a test tube. Ply Alice with questions. Whittle it down to some size that I could understand. I could hardly wait to see Alice alone to analyze further all that I had learned.

We talked a bit longer then went to Nadia's room to see the dresses and fine gifts Yousef had brought her. Finally it was time to say, "good-bye." We reluctantly climbed into the taxi one of the small boys had gotten for us and waved until the taxi turned the corner and they were lost to view.

Back in the small parlor at home I led Alice to the same straight chair and begged her to stay a few minutes longer. "I want to ask you some questions," I said, as I closed the window and pulled the drapes. As it was getting dark early I lit the lamp though it was still an hour before dinnertime.

I sat down on the sofa and leaned forward. "How did you know that would happen to Nadia?" I questioned.

"I didn't know anything." Alice said simply.

"You said that God showed you it would happen. How did He show you, and how did you know it was from God? How were you so sure it would happen just that way?" I threw the questions at her so fast she looked confused and puzzled.

"I thought if I took you and you heard from Nadia and her family. . . ." Alice did not understand my problem.

"Yes, yes," I hurried to reassure her. "I believe it all happened just as you told me, but now I want to know *how* it happened."

"How?" she asked, trying to picture what I couldn't understand. "God simply spoke to me and I knew it would happen."

"Has this always happened to you this way?" I asked, trying to find a question she could answer easily.

"When I was a little girl, no, but after I saw the vision it happened quite often."

"After you saw the vision?" Here was a new element. Instead of a simple answer there was to be more complexity. Alice shifted forward in her chair, and I was afraid she would go without telling me all I wanted to know.

"Before all the trouble started." Alice spoke hurriedly. "Before 1948 when the Palestinians had to flee from their homes, I had a vision. I saw Jesus. He spoke words of such love, and yet there was a warning. I was to tell everyone the vision. After that, after the vision, many things happened to me that never happened before."

I saw that perhaps the vision held the clue to all that I wanted to know, and I pressed her to tell me more but she shook her head firmly. "I have to get home or my sister will be worried about me. She doesn't want me to be out after dark." She got up quickly and hurriedly said good-bye. I followed her to the door and watched her go down the path toward the gate.

Her sister, I pondered. I hadn't known she had a sister and I didn't even know where she lived.

CHAPTER
4

The rainy season passed quickly and the dry days of summer were almost over before Alice reluctantly agreed to take me to her home and let me meet her sister. It was on a Friday, the Moslem holy day when schools were closed and Alice was free. Friday was also the main visiting day at the hospital and as I stood on the wide veranda of our house waiting for her, I watched with my usual fascination as the large, green gate opened at exactly one o'clock for the masses of relatives who came pouring in to visit patients in the hospital.

There were men in flowing black *abas* and white *kaffiyehs* who had just come from prayer at the mosque. There were women dressed in dull black from their veils down to their small, pointed shoes, and here and there in the crowd were Bedouin women with coins hanging from their headpieces down over their noses and mouths leaving only their eyes mysteriously visible. Some of the *fellahin* (or peasant women) carried babies on one hip or balanced woven baskets precariously on their heads while, all the time, in and out and around them were small boys running and shouting, jumping and climbing, all seeming to come toward me as through the zoom lens on a movie camera.

On this day in late summer, the people walked in clouds of dust while donkey carts and cars with honking horns pushed them from behind. I almost despaired of spotting Alice. Again and again I searched for her face in the crowd, but she was nowhere in sight. I was about to go inside when I noticed a car nosing its way through the gate. Looking more closely, I saw Alice leaning out of the window, pointing at me, and motioning the driver to stop.

I waved and hurried down the steps, making my way through the pushing mass of people. I reached for the car door but found myself borne helplessly on with the crowd. Gradually I worked my way back until, with one great effort, Alice was able to reach through the half-open door and pull me inside. "I brought the taxi so you wouldn't have to walk so far," she said.

Too breathless to answer, I sank back in the seat as the car began to move slowly back through the gate, the driver honking and shouting a path through the mob.

"It was my fault," Alice told the driver over and over again. "You were right. It was too hard to try to go into the hospital compound on Friday afternoon."

Not until we were out onto the main street did the driver seem to be placated. "Where to?" he growled, leaning over the steering wheel and looking into his rearview mirror.

"To Ramal," Alice said confidently, with a smile that never wavered as it met his frown. With screeching tires and blowing dust the taxi took off, leaving the people on each side coughing and waving their fists. On Fridays they were dressed in their best.

Though Alice had told me a great deal about her childhood in Jerusalem, she had never before invited me to her home. I had learned that since her mother's death she had lived with her married sister, except for the year after she had been baptized and had become a member of our small Baptist congregation. Then even her sister had turned against her and she had been put out of the house and forced to make other living arrangements. I had subconsciously imagined her sister and her sister's husband as being cold, insensitive people. "You're back now, living with your sister?" I asked.

"Well, yes and no," Alice said, with the usual reluctance to discuss her family situation.

"Is this the same sister you played with as a little girl in Jerusalem?"

"Yes—Melia. There were only three of us, George, Melia, and

I. You know Melia." She said the last words looking at me and enjoying my amazement.

"I know your sister?" I was as surprised as she had known I would be. Quickly I thought of the women I knew and realized that not one of them could be Alice's sister. How could I possibly know her sister? She must be mistaken.

"Yes, you know her and when you see her you will recognize her. You just haven't realized that she is my sister." Alice was obviously enjoying my puzzlement, and when I asked more questions she simply shook her head and said again, "You know her quite well. Just wait. You will see."

We flew past the familiar shops, down past the Tel Azhur hospital, past Suk Faras and the wicker store, on toward the beach where lovely villas lined the quiet streets of the Ramal quarter. The sights outside the window were so familiar I no longer noticed anything. My thoughts were all concentrated on the bits and pieces of her childhood in Jerusalem that Alice had shared with me.

I remembered that she had mentioned a sister, but I had always assumed that it was someone I didn't know. Who could it be? Where could I have met Alice's sister without knowing it? I went over and over in my mind the information I had gleaned of Alice's past. There wasn't much. She didn't talk about herself. Questions were usually answered with a stark "yes" or "no." Only at times would she launch into a story that revealed something of her past and then she usually spoke only of the happy days before the trouble of 1948.

I knew that her father had had a responsible position with the British government. They seemed to have been a very close-knit family living in the well-known, "new," section of Arab Jerusalem called Saad Wa Said.

Her father had a great love for his three children and often took them with him to church or to the *suk* (market). Alice remembered vividly how he would take her by the hand and walk through the Damascus Gate into the old city on his way to the market to buy groceries for dinner. Alice loved the sights and smells of the *suk*. There were always fish lying in shimmering rows on green beds of parsley, their glazed, marble-like eyes cold and unseeing. There were chickens bunched together in tight cane cages, with beady eyes and ruffled feathers, squawking and flapping their wings. Rice, garlic, onions, and flour burst out of huge woven baskets while fresh fruits and vegetables were piled in abundant array.

Always her father chose each purple eggplant or round green cabbage or large Jaffa orange with great care and deliberation. Sometimes he would let Alice choose. On such occasions her eyes would wander over the vegetables as though it were a game she was playing, and at the very last moment she would triumphantly choose the best cabbage or orange in the pile.

Coming home with the full basket was almost as much fun. Her father would set the basket down on the marble counter in the kitchen and her mother would pull out the various purchases, exclaiming over the size, shape, and quality, then finally decide just what she was going to cook for the main meal of the day at two o'clock.

Usually the same menus appeared over and over again in a predictable pattern. Two days of the week they would eat rice with lamb, two days fish, and two days chicken. There was always a day on which they ate only beans. Always she would look for the fruit or vegetable that Alice had picked and then, smiling, she would hug the little girl and say, "You are our special blessing."

On the days her father was in a hurry and could not take Alice to the market, there was still the joy of anticipation. On these days her father would set out early in the morning, stop by the *suk* on his way to work, make his choices, and pay a boy to deliver the produce. When it arrived Alice would sit with her mother and pull from the basket perhaps a large cauliflower, then a bundle of rice tied with a string, and some pieces of lamb wrapped in newsprint. "Father wants fried cauliflower and *mahloobi*," Alice would surmise.

There was a pleasant sameness to the days. Both her father and mother rose early, dressed for the day, and then had their morning prayer and reading from the large family Bible. Only when the boy arrived from the ovens with the daily supply of fresh, warm bread were the children awakened for breakfast.

Alice seemed to especially remember the cold winter days when her mother would unlock the shutters, opening the windows to let in the warm rays of the morning sun. It was warm in the shaft of sunlight, and by the time the children were dressed in their snug, home-knit woolen sweaters they had stopped shivering. George, Melia, and Alice would hurry to their places around the table and wait impatiently for the grace to be said before they could sit down and reach for the steaming hot bread.

Their mother always made bread in the evening, let it rise during the night, and then sent it by a boy to the outdoor ovens. Before daylight he would return with it just in time for breakfast. Usually they dipped pieces of it in olive oil and then in *zatar* or *duhah* (dry, powdered spices), but Alice especially liked the times when there would be a boiled egg for her to hold in her hand until her fingers were warm. There were always plenty of small, tart, green olives with the salty taste of brine and lemon still clinging to them, but best of all was the snow-white *leban* they spread on their bread in great piles and then topped with fig or apricot jam.

Since her family were Greek Orthodox Christians, the holidays were special times that called for new clothes and appropriate food, with something extra for visitors and the poor. Christmas had its Christmas tree and small gifts, while at Easter there were new clothes for everyone and the service in the Church of the Holy Sepulchre. George went with his father to the local tailor for his new suit, but Melia and Alice went with their mother to the home of one of the nearby dressmakers. There, after much deliberation, their mother would order the Palm Sunday dresses and then the ones for Easter. The dresses were always white. Alice remembered that the dresses were soft and satiny and their hair ribbons matched their dresses exactly. To complete the new outfit their father would take them all to the shoe store for new shoes.

More than any other day of the year Alice loved Easter. Alice remembered that the whole family would walk down the long steps that led from the upper *suk* to the Church of the Holy Sepulchre, stopping only briefly for their mother to bring out potatoes, eggs, or bread for the poor beggars that lined the stairs crying pitifully for *baksheesh.* "We could not enjoy all of our blessings if we did not share them with these who have nothing," their mother said as she hurried them along to join the mass of people crowding into the church.

"My father always wanted us to see everything," Alice said, remembering one special Easter and how he had managed to get them right in the center of things. On each side of the entryway to the sepulcher was a balcony surrounded by a filigree network of wrought iron. There were two nuns sitting on the balcony, and when they saw how eager the father was for the little girls to be able to see, they offered to let the girls come up and sit with them where they would be able to see without getting their pretty dresses crushed in the crowd.

"My father lifted us up, and we stood in the darkness holding our candles, seeing only dimly the crowding people below us. Every Easter it was a tradition for a priest to enter the tomb and deliver the holy fire to the waiting people. There was a moment when everyone waited expectantly, then suddenly there would be a burst of flame from the round opening in the side of the marble tomb. 'The holy fire . . . the holy fire,' everyone gasped. Those closest to the tomb lit their candles and then reached back to light the candles of those standing behind them. To us it was always a magical moment, first the burst of flame and then the moving flow of light as candles were lit all over the church."

"There, reach down and light your candle," one of the nuns spoke with a heavy Greek accent to Alice as she helped her reach down over the balcony and light her candle from that of her father.

Alice saw his face tan and handsome in the light of his candle and then her mother, eyes closed, holding her candle with both hands, her lips moving in prayer. "I felt such love for them I thought my heart would break," Alice said. "I wanted it to always be like this one night, all of us together and happy."

Always when Alice talked to me about the past she would stop here, her face would cloud and it was obvious she didn't want to remember any further. I had learned that some time after this her father died and the family fled to Egypt to escape the troubled days of 1948. Somehow this was all connected with the vision. "It was after the vision," Alice would always say as though that was some great dividing line that separated one period of her life from another.

The taxi stopped before a walled villa that had an overgrown look. The large carob trees with dusty leaves loomed over the wall and hid the house from view. The gate was open, and we entered and walked a short distance up the path before it became obvious that the house was large and impressive. The porch was tiled with the colorful terrazzo tiles especially made in Gaza, and there were cane chairs that looked comfortable and used. The windows were open behind the iron grillwork. The sharp, staccato voice of a radio reporter from Cairo filled the air.

Alice rang the bell and I looked at her in amazement. I had not imagined that she lived in such a fashionable district or in such a large, almost elegant, house. It was obvious that Melia had married into a family with means, and again I tried to think of any place I could have met her. "Alice, are you sure I know your sister?" I asked again.

"She's coming. Don't worry, you will see."

A key turned in the lock and the door opened. At first the woman spoke out of the shadows in a soft musical voice, "Come in, come in. What kept you so long?" She moved out into the bright sunlight, and I was astounded to see that she was indeed someone I knew quite well.

"I didn't know. You never told me." I stammered as I looked from one to the other in surprise.

Melia hugged me and kissed me on both cheeks, "You never guessed that I was Alice's sister?" she asked smiling. "I thought Alice would tell you. I just assumed that you knew."

I looked at Alice who turned away rather than meet my questioning gaze. I did indeed know her sister. She was one of the few

Palestinians who was invited with her husband to many of the United Nations parties. I always looked for her and sat by her, talking of our mutual families and friends and never once imagining that this beautifully dressed, perfumed, and jeweled woman was the sister of Alice.

I followed her into the formal parlor and sat on a Victorian-style sofa from Cairo and watched her fling back the curtains and open the shutter-like windows to let in the fresh air and sunlight. Everything was expensive and in good taste. The teacups and warm tea were brought by a young servant, and the tea cakes were delicious.

Alice was unusually quiet, and it was only when I stood and announced that I must go and see where Alice lived that I noticed her tea had not been touched and the small tea cake lay on the saucer without even one bite out of it. It was very strange. Melia was as outgoing and friendly as I had remembered, and yet in her presence Alice became quiet and withdrawn. I remembered with difficulty that this was the same sister that I had always imagined as being so cruel. It seemed impossible.

I repeated all of the polite, Arabic phrases I could remember and Melia answered them with genuine warmth. Time flew. I was once again out in the yard and Alice was waiting for me. "Alice," I said, "I thought you were going to show me your room. I really came to see you, not your sister."

For a moment Alice looked puzzled. Then she nodded and pointed toward the back of the house, "You thought I had a room in the house? No, I'm living out back in what was the small shed where the laundrywomen used to do the weekly wash. It's a big shame and I'm embarrassed but. . . ." I thought I detected a slight quiver in her voice, but the next minute she was pushing back the vines that grew over the path and leading the way to her room.

CHAPTER
5

It had been difficult for Alice to describe where she lived. Now I understood. On first glimpse it looked like a rather nice toolshed sitting close to the high wall that enclosed both the house and yard. As we walked toward the door we had to duck under the wide branches of a fig tree, and I was uncomfortably aware that my shoes were filling with sand. The key turned easily in the lock and Alice remarked, "All of these houses here in the Ramal Quarter near the beach have sandy yards. It's good for growing fruit trees but difficult to walk in."

It was dark inside but when my eyes became accustomed to the dim light I noticed that Alice had tried hard to make the most of this dismal little room. Her single bed, pushed up against the wall took up most of the space. Beside the bed was a small bedside table and chair. The table was covered with an embroidered piece while her Bible and some pictures were arranged on top.

Under her bed were boxes containing the rest of her belongings while over in a corner were some pots and pans stacked neatly beside a small primus stove. I looked for another door leading to a bathroom or for some sort of sink but there was none. This was, as Alice had told me, a regular laundry room such as had been built behind many of the better houses in Gaza. It was built with only one spigot near the cement floor and this was considered quite adequate for a laundry room. I was amazed. I could not imagine how Alice had managed to heat water for bathing or washing dishes or how she had cooked the variety of dishes she had brought me. For a moment I was speechless, and I could see that Alice was embarrassed as she urged me to sit in the one chair that was almost hidden in the corner of the room.

Always the good hostess, she took a cup from under the bedside table and poured me warm, fragrant tea from a vacuum bottle she had obviously prepared earlier. I said, "No thank-you," to the sugar and cream but took a piece of the chocolate candy wrapped in gold paper she offered me from the tin of sweets. I knew how expensive the candies were, and I was impressed that she kept something that special for her guests.

She was watching me closely. I knew that she had not wanted me to see her room or the hurt she felt at Melia's unfeeling rejection, but now that I was here, she wanted my acceptance.

"I am an embarrassement to Melia," she explained. "First of all because I never wanted to get married. This wasn't a problem as long as my mother and father were alive or even after my father's death when I lived with my mother and took care of her, but when she died I had no place to go. Single women can't live alone in Gaza and so I had to come live with Melia."

"Then you could have gotten married, but you chose to remain single?"

"Oh yes, the family is still coming up with rich, old men they want me to marry, and I suppose Melia thinks I am just being stubborn not to marry one of them."

"Did the family choose Melia's husband for her?"

"Yes, in a way I suppose they did. In those days and even now that was the way it was done. Of course Melia was very young."

"Was that when you were in Jerusalem?"

"Yes, we were still in Jerusalem, and Melia and I were playing together out in the yard when a gentleman came to visit. My mother called Melia into the house. She was gone only a short time, and when she came back she was wearing a bunch of gold bracelets. 'See what that nice man gave me.' she said jingling her bracelets. 'He wants to marry me.' That was all she said, and then we continued with our game.

"How old was she?"

"She must have been about thirteen. That sounds young, but it was not unusual in the 1940s to marry at a young age."

"Did Melia stay in Jerusalem?"

"No she came here to live in Gaza, and though Jerusalem wasn't very far away she almost never came to visit."

"Melia didn't want to come home?"

"Oh no, just the opposite. She begged to stay with us. Soon after the wedding Melia and her husband's family stopped to visit on their way to Lebanon for a holiday. Melia wanted to stay with us, and they were very upset by her tears and pleading."

"Did Melia get to stay?"

"Of course not. They made her go. The last thing we saw of Melia was her tear-streaked face as they pulled away. It was so sad."

"Do you think that is why you have never wanted to marry?"

Alice turned away and reached for one of the pictures on the little night table, and I knew I had asked a question she didn't want to answer. "No, I have always wanted to teach school. I never wanted a husband; I only wanted to take care of my mother and father. See, this is my father."

The picture she held out for me to see was of a man and his wife, sitting rather uncomfortably, looking straight into the camera without smiling. The woman was obviously a Palestinian but the man puzzled me. Though he was dark and of medium height, he was somehow different. "Your father was an Italian?" I asked.

"No, he was Greek." Alice said, reaching for the picture and replacing it with another one of what appeared to be twin boys.

"Somehow I had assumed your father was Palestinian."

"No, he was Greek. My great, great-grandfather came from Greece. His name was Stavro and he was a very talented artist. Mohammed Ali, the ruler of Egypt, asked for the best artist to decorate his palace and government buildings and my great, great-grandfather was his choice. He gave him a house and lots of gold. My father's family is rich. I can remember as a little girl going to visit my grandfather in Egypt and seeing a wooden chest filled with gold sitting in one of his back rooms."

"But your father's name was Najeeb Antone. That isn't Greek."

"When my father married my mother who was a Palestinian, and moved to Jerusalem, he changed his name. It was Nicola in Egypt."

"Was your father rich, too?"

"No, not really. He would have been if he had gotten his inheritance from his father. When my grandfather died, my father was sick and couldn't go to the funeral and our relatives in Egypt divided everything among themselves, leaving him out. Soon after that he died and we had nothing. My mother couldn't work. We were all very young. Sometime I will tell you about that time. It was after the vision."

"After we left Jerusalem, we nearly starved to death. I almost died of a kidney infection, but we survived. God took care of us. Oh, sometimes we had only one potato to eat all day, but finally I learned to knit so I could earn a little money. I'm not sure the knitting was very good, but some ladies wanted to help us and they knew we were too proud to accept help, so they taught me to knit and then bought the things I made. As I remember the lumpy scarves and peculiar sweaters I knitted, I realize those ladies must have just been doing that to help us."

Again Alice held out the picture of the two boys. "These are the sons of my cousin in Egypt. There is an interesting story about them. Do you have time to hear it?"

I looked at my watch and saw that it was getting late. I should already be on my way home. I hesitated. If I missed hearing the story now when Alice was ready to tell it perhaps I would never hear it. "Mahmoud will have the table set when I get home so go ahead and tell me the story." I said.

Alice put the picture down and reached for the tin of candy and offered me another piece. When I refused she picked out a large piece wrapped in shiny red paper and insisted. I shook my head, but she unwrapped it and urged me to take it. I knew Alice would not be able to start the story until I had accepted her hospitality, so I finally took it and settled back in the chair. She sat on the edge of the bed and picked up the picture of the two boys.

"My cousin had two girls and then for ten years had no more children at all. She was very upset because, like all Easterners, she worried about her girls. Who would look after them when she and her husband were gone? What if they married men who were not good to them? They needed a brother. 'Pray,' she told me, 'Pray that I will have a son who can take care of his sisters.' "

"That night when I went home I told my mother. She always had a great deal of faith, so she encouraged me. 'She is right. The girls do need a brother to take care of them in the future. It is right to pray for this.' "

"When I went to bed that night I prayed and asked that my cousin would have a son, and in the night I dreamed a dream. I saw an angel, very tall and very fair. He was barefoot and wore a robe with unusually long sleeves. 'Don't be afraid, I am Gabriel,' he said.

"His long sleeves fell back, and in his hands I saw two babies. 'These are for your cousin.' he said. 'The one on the right is named Askander and the one on the left Azziz. Tell your cousin she must name them these names. They will both be blessed, but one of them will be rich and very successful.'

"When I told my mother, she decided that I should go and tell my cousin the whole dream just as I had seen it. I went that same morning to my cousin's house and told her, but she could not believe that after all this time she could possibly have a baby boy, let alone twins. 'What shall I do with twins?' my cousin said.

"Don't forget to name them Askander and Azziz. That is important." Alice told her. She insisted that her cousin get a piece of paper and write down the names so she wouldn't forget them. Reluctantly, the cousin got the paper and wrote the names. She didn't believe there would actually be twins born to her but she did it to humor Alice.

Soon after this Alice, her mother, and George left Egypt and moved to Gaza. The prediction about the twins was forgotten in all the confusion of getting settled in a new place. Then, one day two years later when one of the cousins was visiting Gaza he said, "You will be interested to know my sister has had twin boys and she has named them Askander and Azziz. At first we were puzzled by the names, but my sister told us about the dream. It is hard to believe but she insists it's true."

"You will see when they are older," Alice told him. "The rest of the prediction will come true. One of them will be very rich."

Alice got up as though the story were finished, but I still sat looking at the picture of the two young boys. It did seem a bit strange that Alice had first seen them in a dream with Gabriel holding them. No wonder her cousin had been so surprised. I would have found it hard to believe if I had not been actually holding the picture in my own hands. The picture seemed to represent some sort of solid, visible proof. I found myself wondering if this was also another one of those strange, inexplicable miracles that began to happen after she saw the vision she was always referring to.

"This also happened after the vision?" I asked Alice as I got up and moved toward the door.

"Oh yes, I saw the vision in Jerusalem after we fled into Egypt." She took the picture I handed her and opened the door.

It was too late to ask her more about the vision or the twins. The sun was hanging low over the Mediterranean, waiting to drop from sight at any minute, and the new, crescent moon already rode high in the sky. I would barely get home before supper time.

The cab rounded the far corner but neither Alice nor I spoke. I was too lost in thought. Here was another strange happening that I couldn't quite fit comfortably into my philosophy. "Alice," I asked, "Is one of the boys rich?"

She smiled. "Yes, one of them is quite rich."

"Which one?" I asked as the taxi pulled up beside us.

"Azziz is the rich one." Alice said matter-of-factly.

I didn't know really what difference it made whether Askander or Azziz was richer, but somehow it was part of the whole strangeness of her story. I probably never would actually see the twins or talk to their mother, but I had seen the photograph. I would have to accept the story just as it was. I had no way to examine it further, but I wanted to.

By the time I reached home I had made up my mind that as soon as possible I was going to get Alice to tell me about the vision. The vision seemed to be central to everything I could not understand. Perhaps the vision would at least give me some clue as to how all of this started.

CHAPTER
6

Several weeks went by and I was no closer to hearing the story of the vision than I had been before. The days were getting shorter. The rains had started, and though Alice came every day to visit patients or stopped by my house, she never had time to stay and talk. "Don't be impatient," she always said, "I am going to tell you the vision, but it will take time."

When the day finally came it was no different than most other days. "Alice is looking for you," I was told by one of the nurses. I had just finished teaching the children, so I decided to go to the hospital's sewing room. Alice usually stopped there to visit with her friend Sitt Huddah. Sitt Huddah lived at the hospital. She had been there long before when the British owned the hospital. She told Bible stories to children in the hospital and visited patients.

Late afternoons in the hospital's small sewing room were pleasant times even in the bitter cold of the winter rains. With its two humming machines, piles of gowns and sheets to be mended, and bright laughter it was everyone's favorite meeting place. Young nurses coming off duty and students carrying books back to their rooms across the hall would stop to warm themselves by the tall kerosene heater and to chat. As shifts and classes changed, nurses and students moved in and out. There were only brief periods when Sitt Huddah and the seamstresses were left alone to greet the newcomers.

"*Ahlan, ahlan,*" Sitt Huddah said as I opened the door and asked if any of them had seen Alice.

Madeline, a student nurse from Egypt, pulled out a chair and urged me to sit down, "I saw Alice over in the hospital visiting one of the children from her class in school," she said.

"*Uhuddi, uhuddi*" (sit down), Sitt Huddah urged as she rocked gently back and forth, a smile flitting across her face and her sightless eyes looking straight ahead.

"I have only a few minutes," I said as I sank into the chair and held my cold hands out over the heater. "It's Bible study night. I have to be sure Mahmoud gets the chairs set up in the living room."

"I like your new drapes." Madeline said as she peeled an orange and offered me one of the bright juicy sections.

"There are so many windows I had to buy all the material the man had in his shop. I wasn't sure how blue roses would look but it was all I could find that would do at all."

"I liked it and so did the other girls," Madeline said. "It would look nice on our beds, but there wasn't any more like it left in the shop."

I had to laugh. "I'm sure it would look better on your beds than as drapes in my living room, but in Gaza you have to manage with what you can find."

The sweet smell of toasting orange peel filled the room as Madeline put the curling rinds on the hot metal of the heater. "Should I come and get you for the meeting tonight?" Madeline asked Sitt Huddah.

There was a moment of silence as Sitt Huddah rocked gently back and forth while her fingers twisted and untwisted a white handkerchief. "No, Alice has offered to come get me." Sitt Huddah said as she ran her fingers along the hem of her handkerchief.

I got up to leave, thinking how thoughtful it was of Alice to notice that Sitt Huddah needed help to get places. Even though she was blind she spent a lot of time telling stories to children in the hospital and visiting families in the warren of houses that crowded close around the back gate, but wherever she went someone had to go with her. She was quite helpless in many ways. Even going to the dining room for her meals was a great effort.

I hurried down the winding stone steps letting my hand slide along the cold length of the wrought iron rail, *I'm glad,* I thought, *that Sitt Huddah has a friend like Alice and it is good for Alice,* too. *They need each other.*

As I passed the door of the outpatient clinic I noticed that there were only a few patients left to be seen and Subhi had already begun mopping the floor. I came out into the large courtyard in front of the chapel and saw Alice but decided not to disturb her. She was listening intently to something a young woman was telling her. The woman was crying and had obviously just pulled back the cloth covering a sick child that lay motionless in her lap. Alice didn't see me, and I hurried on past the formal garden to my own back door.

I quickly checked the living room and found the chairs were in place for the Bible study, the songbooks stacked on a table near the door. Everyone, doctors, nurses, and our own children enjoyed the Wednesday-night Bible study. It was a time for favorite songs and choruses in both Arabic and English and then twenty minutes of Bible study taught by one of the doctors while Ed Nicholas, our pastor, and his family were at home in the States.

It had grown dark early and I switched the light on to look around the room. In the daytime the blue roses on the yards and yards of cotton draperies were muted and shaded, but at night when the lights were on they took on a life of their own that was almost overpowering. I noted the chairs near the front where Sitt Huddah and Alice usually sat. Maybe I could persuade Alice to stay after the meeting and tell me about the vision. One of the nurses would be glad to see that Sitt Huddah got back to her room.

The meeting ended early and the children went upstairs with David for a good-night story while I said the usual good-byes. I turned out the lights in the big parlor and hurried across the hall to the small reception room. Alice was already there waiting for me, and I could tell by the way she was leaning back in the green chair that she had decided to tell me about the vision.

She was strangely quiet, and I realized that this was not something she talked about easily. I got the kerosene heater as the room was damp and cold. Alice seemed used to the cold of the Gaza rainy season but I was always shivering in the huge, unheated house. I grabbed a woolen throw and curled up at the end of the sofa nearest the heater. "You are going to tell me about the vision," I said studying her face that was half hidden in the shadows.

She didn't answer but instead leaned forward and looked for what seemed a long time into the glowing flames behind the grate of the heater. When she started to tell the story it was almost as though she was reliving the whole experience and I wasn't even there.

"The first thing I remember," she said as she began the story, "was coming into the small garden at the side of our house in Jerusalem. It was early morning and very dark. To my surprise, the large family Bible was out of its usual place in my father and mother's room and instead was lying open in the basement window. I was shocked. I felt it would soon be three o'clock in the morning and my mother and father would be getting up as they did every morning to have their devotional together. What would they think when they found their Bible missing?

"I ran forward and was about to pick up the Bible when I was blinded by a great light and heard a voice saying, 'Come, my dear, I want to tell you many things because the time is near.' I looked to see where the voice was coming from and saw only light, brilliant light, like fireworks of blue and green but very bright. I was terribly afraid. I ran as fast as I could back into the house.

"I don't know how much time passed before I again found myself back in the garden. This time I heard a voice that was very soft and kind, full of love, saying, 'Don't be afraid my darling; come to me because I want to tell you many things to tell the people because the time is short.'

"Slowly, I went toward the voice, but I didn't dare look up. I saw only a glowing white robe and feet that were wearing sandals. Gradually I gained confidence and looked up. I saw that it was a man and he was very beautiful. He didn't look like any of the pictures I had ever seen. 'Look at my hands and my feet,' he said. 'I was crucified on the cross for you and for all the people.' I looked and saw that it was as he said, on his hands and feet there were nail holes and the blood was still to be seen.

"I knew it was Jesus. I fell to my knees and began to weep. Immediately he spoke again, 'Don't cry, my darling, because you are doing all the things that please me. You will have blessings in heaven and on earth.'

"He reached down and took the Bible and opened it to 1 Thessalonians 3:13 and chapter 4. He put his hand on these verses, and I noticed that they were all in big letters. 'Read here,' he said, 'so you will be comforted. There will be great suffering in all countries but if you remember these words you will be comforted.'

"When I had finished reading, he said, 'Read also the Book of Revelation. I want you to tell the people to pray and to read the Bible, especially Revelation. Don't be ashamed, my dear, if they refuse to listen and even laugh at what you say. The world does not know me, and the believers are few and the sinners many.'

" 'You will suffer much for my sake. Be patient until the end, so you will have blessings in heaven and on earth.

'Tell the people, my dear, to repent because the time is very near. Don't forget, my sister, to tell the people the time is very near and to take the Holy Bible with you.' With that he handed me the Bible and a great happiness filled my heart. I began to read and sing with joy.

"It was early in the morning when I knocked on my parents' door. They were surprised at what I told them, and they began to exclaim over the strange glow that seemed to radiate from my face like it had oil on it. I took the Bible and read the section He had pointed out to me and we marked it. 'He told me to warn all the people because the time is short and there will be great suffering,' I said. 'I don't know how to do what he asked. I am just a young girl, and they will laugh at me.'

"My parents immediately decided to pray about it, and then they said that we should all go talk to Mr. Roy Whitman who was preaching at that time in one of the churches. I was so afraid, but he encouraged me and I got up after the church service on the next Sunday and told about the vision. After that, I was asked to go many places, even where there were visitors from other countries and they brought a translator to translate. Often when there was a conference in Jerusalem they would ask me to come and tell about the vision.

"Finally a printer named Khalil Gabriel printed the story, and it was distributed all over Palestine. I signed it only A.N.A. because I didn't want to seem proud. It was strange but when people would read the little tract they would often ask, 'Who is A.N.A.?' and when they found out that I was just a young girl they would ask me to come and tell about the vision in my own words.

"It stirred up a lot of controversy in the Arab community; many people scoffed, 'The war is over,' they said. 'The Turks are no longer here to oppress us and the British are going to find a solution to all our problems. How can there be the trouble you are telling us about?'

"I would have to shake my head and say I didn't know. I was only repeating what had been told me in the vision.

"At the same time many people were laughing there were others who confessed their sins and got right with God."

Alice leaned back in the chair and I knew that she had told me all she intended to tell but there were so many questions left unanswered. "What year did you have the vision?" I asked, remembering all the trouble that began for the Arabs at the time of the partition of Palestine in 1948.

"It was before my brother George was sick or my father had died, so it must have been about 1943."

I had never heard much about George and so I asked, "Did your brother die?"

"No, no," she said. "It was just that he was very sick and in the hospital. The doctors had even put him out on the porch to die, and my father was getting ready to call the hospital when he heard God's voice say, 'Believe me, your son is healed.' He said it three times. At that moment the phone rang and it was the doctor saying that George was all right and they had put him back in the room with the other children.

"But your father did die?" I asked. I had never heard her mention this before.

"Yes, his death changed everything for my family. We had only his small pension, and it wasn't enough to buy food and pay for the rooms. My mother went to the sisters at the Dom Polskey's convent in the old city of Jerusalem and told them her problem. They were so kind. 'There is a woman with a baby who works in our kitchen,' the sister said. 'She needs a place to live and the money she pays will help you feed your children.'

"Even though I had been warned in a dream that my father would die, still I could not accept it. I cried, refused to eat, and sincerely wanted to die. I thought there was nothing that could ever heal the grief I felt for my father, but then something happened. Something strange and wonderful happened that instantly comforted me and changed my whole feeling about his death."

"I was sitting at home, by myself, reading my Bible when suddenly my father appeared before me. 'Why are you crying?' he asked.

" 'I am crying because you died,' " I told him.

"He sat down beside me and in a very loving voice said, 'But I am not dead; I am in glory.' "

" 'What do you mean by 'glory?' "I asked.

" 'Wait,' he said. 'I'll show you.'

"Then a wonderful thing happened. I saw my father by the side of Jesus and again there was much light flashing, all blue and green, with angels and people like Abraham. There was beautiful singing, and my father nodded to me and it all faded, but I never cried for him again."

We sat for a few moments in total silence. I understood why it had taken Alice such a long time to tell me of the vision. Actually, it now appeared there was not just one vision but many. She was reluctant to tell people who were so skeptical they would only criticize or laugh.

I wanted to ask a thousand questions, but I knew I must be careful lest Alice think I did not understand. "Had this kind of thing always happened to you?" I asked finally.

"Never, I never had a vision until after I saw Jesus and received the warning. But after that many things happened. Three years before my father died I had a dream in which I saw a large black bird that walked around in a circle three times and there was a voice that said, 'In three years your father will die.' I cried and when my father came in to be sure we were covered for the night he asked why I was crying and I told him about the dream. He was not upset. Instead, he tried to comfort me but I knew the dream was true.

"Have you had warnings like this often?" I asked.

"Yes. There was at this time another strange thing that happened. The night before my father died I saw a big clock and the hands were stopped at seven. The cars stopped in the streets and everything was dead and still. All the people asked who had died, and I knew it was the clock of death. The same thing happened before my mother died. I had the same dream."

We sat looking at the warm glow of the kerosene heater. While the shadows danced and flickered on the pale walls and rose-patterned drapes, each of us thought our own thoughts. It was late. Alice would have to be going, and there were so many things I wanted to ask. "Alice," I said, "What is the difference between a dream and a vision?"

She thought about it for awhile and then said, "I suppose some would call the experience I had with the Bible and seeing Jesus a dream, but it was too real to be an ordinary dream. In the middle when I became frightened and ran away, I actually went out into the kitchen where my mother was squeezing lemons. I got a drink of water and went back to bed, but my trip to the kitchen seemed no more real than my return to the small garden where I again encountered Jesus."

"Were you really out of bed and in the small garden?" I asked.

"It was so real I would have said I was out in the garden, but I awoke in my bed with my hands clasped as though in prayer and my knees bent as though kneeling."

"Did all the trouble really come as Jesus said it would?"

Alice stood up and reached for her coat. "I have to go now.

There is no time to tell of what happened after that." At the door she stopped and grew serious, "Trouble, yes there was trouble that came. We could not even have imagined at that time the trouble that was coming to our own family and to all of Palestine"

I knew from experience that she wouldn't tell me any more. A friend was waiting to drive her home and she had to hurry. To my surprise she stopped at the front door and turned back, "Before I came over to the service tonight I was talking to a woman at the hospital today whose only child had fallen from a third-story window. The little boy was unconscious and the father had gone to get one of the doctors."

"Yes, I know," I said, "I saw you talking to her."

"Did you see how the mother was crying? The baby was completely limp, barely breathing." Alice had the door open and was ready to hurry out to the car. "I prayed for the little boy in Jesus' name and then told the mother, 'He'll be all right. Tomorrow he will speak and the next day you can take him home.'"

As Alice hurried down the steps and across the walk to the car I tried to keep up with her. "Alice, how could you encourage her that way. What if it doesn't happen?"

Alice was in the car leaning out the window smiling, "Mrs. Dorr, you will see. You must have faith."

Old Ablabed closed the gate and I lingered by his charcoal fire warming my hands. He had a blackened copper coffeepot balanced on the coals and his small, half-finished cup of coffee sitting on the bench. I deliberately determined to forget the vision and Alice's strange encounter with the woman and her unconscious child. I'd think of that tomorrow. Right now it was enough to greet the kindly old man and thank him for being so patient with the children.

I had seen him let the little boys hold on to the cross-bars of the gate and ride half circle as it opened. Countless times I had discovered that he had let them eat part of his dinner of bread and *zatar*. On warm summer nights he didn't scold when the pajama-clad John slipped out of bed to sit beside his fire. He always gave him a small cup of coffee and sang in his old cracked voice *"Tiddlum, tiddlum, ba, bu, ba."*

As I turned up the walk I could hear the motor of the car throbbing as it waited a moment to turn out onto the main street. There were no other noises at this hour. The streets were deserted. Even the coffee shop across the street was silent and dark. From the front porch I noticed that there was one shaft of light from the operating room at the hospital, and I knew that David had found it necessary to operate on the man he had been concerned about at dinner.

Medicine was such an exact science. Everything was logical, nothing mysterious. It was easy to deal with, while Alice and her promise to the woman that her only son would be healed made me uneasy and fearful. I almost wished she would stop seeing people and praying for them. Surely there would come a time when she would be wrong and someone would have their faith in God destroyed.

I shut the door behind me and stood in the dark hallway. *But,* I thought, *if it had been one of my boys that fell from the window, how would I feel?* All my pretensions fell away and I knew I would pray and would welcome anyone else who was on such intimate terms with God and His will.

CHAPTER
7

I had gotten the Calvert Course tests back and was looking over them to see what comments those distant teachers' helpers in Baltimore had to make. It was easy to go astray when I was the children's only teacher. As far as I could figure, each child was behind at least one year through no fault of their own. First the books hadn't arrived for six months and then I had taken time off when our youngest son Jimmy was born. Finally David and I had both come down with severe cases of hepatitis that kept us in bed for three months and a long recuperation after that.

The tests were rather discouraging. I would have to find a way to bring the children's grades up. Philip's especially. In the fall he would be going to Beirut where he would stay in the home of David and Maxine King while he attended the American International School. The next spring we would have been in Gaza four-and-a-half years, and it would be time for a furlough in the States. All the children must be prepared to fit into the regular American school system.

I leaned back in the straight dining room chair and warmed my hands on a cup of tea. I didn't like to think about the fall. Our only connection with Beirut and the outside world was the U.N. Caribou that flew twice a week as prescribed by law, ten miles out into the Mediterranean Sea and up the coast avoiding Israel, to Lebanon. There was no other facility for communication, no telephone, mail system, or transportation. Each of us was allowed only two flights out each year, so there was no chance of flying back and forth to check on him once he had gone. I caught myself worrying about it a lot. Philip seemed too young to be so cut off from his family.

I looked at the clock, put the cup down, and picked up my Arabic book. I was to have a lesson at four o'clock that afternoon, and there was a whole paragraph of Arabic to be learned before then. It seemed I was always pushing to get just the basics done.

Eight forty-five came all too soon. I folded up the books, checked with Mahmoud as to the possibilities for lunch and then hurried up the long staircase to the second floor. The children were roller skating in and out of the upstairs bedrooms, which all opened onto a large veranda. We had reluctantly given our permission for the skating because it really didn't hurt the tile floors and everything outside was muddy and wet.

There was extensive pleading to be allowed to keep the skates on during school, but long experience and the recent test grades made the pleas unheeded. The skates were piled in a row outside the door and another school day began.

All this time as my mind was seemingly occupied with the tests and preparation for my Arabic lesson, there had been the constant, nagging fear that somewhere in the hospital things might not be going so well for the little boy who had fallen from the window. Over and over again I pictured the child at the window and then the fall. "Was the house tall?" I wondered. "Was there possibly grass under the window to ease his fall?" I had only caught a glimpse of the mother and the limp, little form that she held, but the picture seemed to be indelibly stamped on my mind.

Along with the picture always came the fear that the child might have died by the time Alice arrived in the afternoon. I knew Alice didn't make rash statements about what God was going to do. I was sure if I asked her, she would tell me, as she had told me before, that as she prayed for the child God had told her he would be healed. I tried to remember her exact words. "Tomorrow he will speak and the next day you can take him home," she had told the mother.

The exact words seemed to be very important. She would always tell me first in Arabic and then in English trying several times

to get the right word in English to express the precise thought. It
had become evident to me that this was no occult mumbo jumbo
but a simple faith and the ability to hear the voice of God so clearly
that she knew what would happen.

The day went quickly. We had actually eaten our supper and it
was getting dark before I realized that Alice wasn't coming. Was
it possible she hadn't come to the hospital at all? Maybe she had
come and the child was dying or dead. I tried to forget the whole
thing and work on the next day's Arabic lesson but the fear would
not go away. *Alice should not have encouraged the mother,* I
thought, finally. *Even if she has been right in every instance I
know about still. . . .*

I folded my papers and closed the book. It was impossible to
concentrate. I would have to go see one of the nurses and ask
about the woman.

I walked the short distance to the hospital noticing the lights
were on in the student nurses' rooms and a soft glow radiated from
each of the small windows in the dining room. I said "Hello," to
Hamdi who always seemed to be in the telephone room putting
calls through with the help of his antiquated box of wires, plugs,
and jangling bells.

I passed the operating room and then the private room, noticing
that both were dark. A few nursing students hurried past with
trays of needles and little cups of pills. They all smiled and murmured a soft Arabic greeting in either an Egyptian or Lebanese
accent.

The foreign nurses, American and Australian, and our one
female doctor lived on the third floor of the hospital. It was to their
apartment I was going. It was still early enough so that most of
them would be working on the wards, and I would be fortunate
to find even one of the Australians at home. If it was Ethne she
wouldn't know about the woman because she was always in the
operating room, but if it was Marian Jenner there was just a chance
that she had been on the children's ward and had seen the little
boy and his mother.

The cold, stone stairway circled up through the center of the hospital to the third floor. It exhibited quite adequately the artistic bent of the British doctors who had built the hospital eighty years before. I loved the charm and symmetry of the stairs, but understood the feelings of Bedouin women who, having lived only in the small, cubical U.N. houses, clung with terror to the wrought iron rail as they tried to descend the stairs on the narrow side.

I found Marian in her room dressed in her warm Australian robe and big, fluffy slippers. She was sitting beside her kerosene heater writing letters. She never wasted a moment, so when she insisted on making tea and serving me some homemade bread and Australian marmalade, I started to decline.

"I was just about to make myself some tea," Marian urged. "I've been so rushed today I haven't really felt like eating anything."

I followed her to the dining-room table and while she put the kettle on I asked about the woman.

"Yes, we've been concerned about the little boy all day, but this afternoon he opened his eyes and recognized his mother."

"Does he seem to be all right? Did he say anything?"

"One never knows about cases like that. It was a bad fall, and it would seem that they will be fortunate if he ever walks again. Yes, he did say something to his mother, and she was so touched she started to cry."

As I went home and found my way up the long stairs and to bed, I thought about the child and his mother. He had talked as Alice said he would, but would he be able to walk or even think of going home the next day? I doubted it. That was asking too much.

David was already asleep, and I dared not wake him because he could be called at any time. I desperately wanted to ask him if it was at all possible for a little boy to fall three stories and suffer no permanent damage. I leaned on my elbow and listened to his rhythmic breathing. I would have to wait. There was no other way. I slid down under the pile of covers and felt for the hot water bottle. The call to prayer echoing and reechoing on the cold damp air would be announcing another day soon enough.

The next day my preoccupation with the whole situation had cooled as I determined Alice was at least half right: the child had said a few words. He was evidently not brain damaged. It was good to come to terms with the situation as I had slept very little, "worrying before the Lord," as David called it. I had noticed that Alice never seemed to go through the agonizing most of us indulge in when we are concerned. She had faith—not faith in what she thought should happen but faith that what God had shown her when she prayed would come to pass.

"Alice wants to see you. She is at the door with a friend." It was late the next afternoon when Philip came bounding up the stairs to the schoolroom with this announcement.

I dropped everything and hurried down the steps to the front door. Through the screen I could see Alice with a small woman who was holding a child, and both of them were smiling. It was so unexpected that at first I didn't say anything.

It was evident that Alice assumed I knew who they were because she just stood and smiled and urged the mother to put the child down. "See," she said, "he can walk."

Slowly it dawned on me that this was the child that had fallen from the window. The child I had been so worried about. I could hardly believe what I was seeing. He was actually walking. The child seemed to be completely well.

"Would you mind," I finally asked, "If I took a picture? I want to remember this."

The picture was quite ordinary. Just a mother looking rather serious because she was having her picture taken and a little boy sitting in her lap. I am always amazed that this is the same mother I saw holding the limp child and weeping.

The woman was in a hurry to leave and so we went through the usual elaborate Arabic "good-byes" I stood and watched her walk through the small garden near the church and out toward the gate.

I put my camera back into its case as my mind whirled with questions. "The woman was Moslem wasn't she?" I finally asked.
"Yes."

"She doesn't believe in Jesus as anything more than a good man or a prophet, so how did you pray?"

Alice was puzzled, "You don't believe Jesus would heal a Moslem?"

"No, I don't really mean that. I just wondered about it since you always pray in Jesus' name."

"When Jesus was here on earth, he healed a lot of Jews who didn't really know very much about Him."

"But isn't faith important?"

Alice hesitated, "Look, I always ask the person if they are right with God. Every person in the world knows if he is right with God. Then I tell them that I pray in Jesus' name, and I ask them if they believe that Jesus can heal them. Most of them believe."

"A Moslem believes that Jesus can heal him?"

"I know that seems strange to you, but the Koran tells of many miracles Jesus performed. It also says that Jesus is alive."

"But they don't believe that Jesus is the Son of God."

"No, and they feel strongly about that because they think that implies that Mary was the wife of God. It is hard for them to understand."

"They don't believe that Jesus died on the cross."

"I know this doesn't make sense but they believe that if Jesus was divine, how could he die? There was an early group of Christians called Nestorians that believed the same thing, and many feel that Muhammad learned everything he knew about Christianity from them."

"Do you pray for many Moslems?"

"Wherever I am called, I go. I only pray; it is God who answers as He chooses."

I was about to say good-bye when Alice reached out and held my arm, "Wait. I have something I must tell you." The smile was gone, and she seemed disturbed.

I was so used to Alice's good humor and faith that I had not imagined anything could upset her. "What's the matter?" I asked, studying her face for clues.

"My sister Melia and her husband are very upset with me."

"Why?"

"They say people are laughing at me."

"Laughing at you! They must be mistaken."

"No. It is true. First because I was baptized and became a Baptist and now because I am praying for people."

"I don't understand."

"I have become an embarrassment to Melia and her husband. They say I have made a spectacle of myself praying for people."

"And they want you to stop praying for people. Is that it?"

For a few moments Alice said nothing. When she finally spoke her face had lost all its bright happiness. "Melia has talked with my relatives in Egypt," her voice was so low I could hardly hear her, "and they have decided I must get married."

"I didn't know there was someone in Egypt you were even interested in marrying." I had never heard any hint of Alice's getting married.

Alice shot me a pained look, "I've never seen him. He's an old man, very rich, and he'll take care of me. 'Control me,' they say. That's all they are interested in. They want someone to take care of me and to manage me."

"But if you don't want to marry him you don't have to. You have a good job and can take care of yourself so why are you so afraid?"

"It is very difficult for a woman to live alone. I know that, but my mother and father promised and Melia promised.

"When is this wedding supposed to take place?"

"When school is out and I go for my vacation to Egypt. They are all upset. They think if they get me away from here and married this will solve all their problems."

"Then," I said, trying to put together all the pieces, "when you get to Egypt this summer they will have the wedding all planned even though you have never met the man?"

"Yes. They have this old man who is looking for a wife. They think it is for the best, but I could not endure such a thing." She gave me one long look to see if I understood and then she quickly said good-bye and left.

Of course, that is how they would solve what seemed to them such a complicated problem. Alice had done several things that were totally against what was usually expected of a woman in Gaza. To teach school was all right, but to make independent decisions such as not agreeing to marriage or to change from the Greek Orthodox Church and go around independently praying for people—this would be unthinkable to someone like Melia.

The whole family felt responsible for Alice, and it would be a relief to them if she were married to a strict husband who would control her. I tried to think what it would mean for Alice. A husband would have every right to lock her in the house and keep her from seeing anyone. He was a complete stranger, but would serve their purpose.

For the first time I had seen Alice worried, and I could easily imagine that it would be almost impossible to stand against the whole family. As difficult as things had been for her living in the small laundry room behind her sister's house, this would be far worse. I knew Alice would pray, but could she be rescued? It seemed improbable.

Surely, I thought. *God will protect her. How could her prayers be answered for others and not for herself?* With that thought in mind, I felt much better even though there remained a nagging concern that this could prove to be far more difficult than I anticipated.

CHAPTER
8

With early summer and school closing, Alice packed to go to Egypt. It would be hot in Cairo, and she knew as soon as she arrived there would be pressure to find a dressmaker, buy material for an engagement or wedding, and go to visit the family of the old man her relatives had picked for her to marry. It would not be a pleasant holiday.

When the day finally came I found myself thinking over all the things Alice had told me about her past experiences in Egypt. I knew she would be remembering the other times she had ridden on this same train down across the Sinai to Cairo. "I never make this trip," Alice told me, "without remembering how it was the first time when my mother with George and I, fled down to Egypt.

"I can remember every detail, as though it were yesterday," Alice said. "It was 1947 and Christmas in Jerusalem. The British were leaving and there was trouble just like the vision had shown. It was all crashing down upon us. Every day brought new horror stories of gun battles and blockades. The Israelis were frantically preparing for war and the Arab armies stood poised, ready at the slightest provocation to march across the border.

"If we were to escape getting caught in the cross fire we would have to leave immediately. There was no time for anything. We had to leave our Christmas tree standing with its string of lights and bright ornaments. The curtains had to be left hanging and none of the furniture moved. The trip itself was hazardous. We could take only the bare necessities, only what we could carry. Of course, that included the large family Bible.

" 'We can't stay here in Jerusalem,' my mother had explained. 'Every day there is news of people being killed, others threatened, and now it is even dangerous to be traveling on the road.'

"I remember my mother gathering us together for prayer, asking God to protect us and bring us safely to our relatives in Egypt. I remember looking at the Christmas tree and the warm, familiar room and thinking how quickly everything had changed. My father's death had been the first blow and now this uprooting. The last thing we did in Jerusalem was to go to the cemetery where my father was buried. We all cried and were still crying when we got into the taxi that would take us to Gaza where we were to catch the train for Egypt.

"I remember vividly every detail of our arrival in Egypt. Instead of welcoming us, my father's relatives were critical and unfeeling. They gave us some rooms in an apartment they owned, but nothing more. There was no heat for the cold January nights and worse yet there were no beds or even blankets. Our food consisted of an occasional boiled potato or a few large rounds of bread.

"It was fortunate that I had learned some English at Miss Radford's house where I often visited and went to Sunday School. In Egypt I made friends with some British women who soon noticed that something was wrong. They knew my mother was too proud to accept help. Even when they asked questions, I dared not answer because my mother had warned us against letting anyone know of our problems.

"In spite of this they must have noticed how difficult things were for our little family and determined to find a way to help. The result was they taught me to knit and promised to buy everything I made. My knitting wasn't very good, but they exclaimed over it and paid me far better than my work deserved." Alice never mentioned this without smiling as though she could vividly remember the ill-fitting garments she had knitted.

"It was awful for my mother." Her face reflected the pain they had endured. "She had lost everything—husband, home, possessions, and income. But with all that there was still more trouble to come. Something happened to me that at the time seemed tragic but turned out to be wonderful. I don't know how to explain it," she would always say. "It was very strange."

Alice was reluctant to discuss what had happened. It was not clear whether it was because those days held such painful memories or because the miracle she experienced was too meaningful to share with people who might not understand. However, this one experience far overshadowed everything else that happened to her in Egypt and she remembered it vividly.

"In the midst of our darkest days," Alice would say, "I became sick. Deathly sick. My back throbbed with an excruciating pain and my fever rose to an alarming degree. It was obviously the old problem I had experienced with my kidneys, only worse.

"There was no money for a doctor or a hospital, let alone for transportation to the hospital. I lay shivering on the floor wrapped in the only blanket my family owned. I felt the sharp, stabbing pain, the aching, and the nausea. I also felt my mother's hand tighten on mine as she prayed, but it all seemed so hopeless. Though we had read daily from the big Bible and prayed, nothing changed. It seemed that heaven was closed. The door was locked and no amount of knocking made any difference.

"There was no money for candles or oil for a lamp, so as darkness settled in I felt completely isolated. Even my mother's voice praying seemed to come from a great distance and finally stopped all together as she left the room and I was alone.

"I don't know how much time passed but suddenly I was aware of someone else in the room. I opened my eyes. In the dim light I saw a man in armor standing in the shadows and I immediately knew it was Saint George. I had seen many pictures of him, since he is the patron saint of the Greek Orthodox Church. The Saint's eyes were kind, and he told me not to be afraid. I would be healed. Then he disappeared.

"The next day I told my mother about seeing Saint George. She was astonished and began questioning me about it. 'What makes you think it was Saint George?' she asked. 'Perhaps it was Jesus who came and you only thought it was Saint George.'

" 'No Mother,' I said. 'I know it was Saint George because of the armor he wore and the horse he had with him.' "

"Horse?' my mother questioned.

" 'Yes,' I told her. 'It was a horse and I remember how it impatiently pawed the ground right near my head.' She didn't know what to think. She probably thought a high fever had triggered my imagination and she wasn't going to be swerved from her determination to get me to the hospital.

"I don't know where she got the money for the tram fare nor do I know how we walked to the tram and managed to get on. I do remember that it was very crowded and we were so squeezed we could hardly breathe.

"At each stop more people got on, and as they pushed and shoved to make room, suddenly a large, fat lady came elbowing her way to where I stood. With one more push she jammed her elbow into my stomach. I bent double and groaned. The pain was excruciating. There was a sudden flood of water and the sound of a small stone hitting the floor and bouncing.

" 'I'm healed, Mother, I'm healed,' I cried, reaching out and around the people that separated us to grab my mother's arm. 'I don't have to go to the hospital. We can go home.'

"My mother was confused. She was even more worried now that she had seen how hard the woman had hit me, and she couldn't believe I was not seriously hurt. She shook her head and insisted we go on to the hospital.

"At the hospital I remember being taken to a small room, given a hospital gown, and told to hang my dress in the cupboard. It was the only dress I had and I was afraid to let it out of my sight for fear that someone would steal it or misplace it. At the same time I didn't want to admit to the nurse that I had only one dress.

"I got into the hospital gown, praying all the time. When the nurse came to get me, I went reluctantly off to have the tests made. The minute I was back in the room I checked the little cupboard and was relieved to find the dress still there, hanging just as I had left it. Hurriedly I put it on and sat on the edge of the bed waiting for the nurse.

"When she finally came she seemed surprised to find me dressed and ready to leave. 'You were right,' she said, 'You must have passed the stone that was causing all the trouble. The doctor says you won't have to have the operation.' "

As difficult as the first trip to Egypt had been, the trip she now faced would be much harder. She would be riding to Egypt alone and facing relatives that were pitted against her. They didn't mean to be unkind. However, they felt responsible for her, and to them the only solution was to arrange a marriage with this wealthy, old man who would take care of her.

When Alice came to say good-bye I could tell she had been crying. Her eyes were red and had dark circles under them. When I asked her where she had been, she was at first reluctant to answer. Finally she admitted, "I have been to my mother's grave." She turned away not wanting me to see the tears that welled in her eyes. "Everything would have been so different if only my mother had lived."

I had often passed the area behind the hospital where the wrought-iron fence separated the Greek Orthodox Church and its crowded cemetery from the crush of houses that filled Gaza's downtown area. The church was old. It had been built in AD 450 and with the passing of time the ground had risen around the church until now its handsome wooden doors opened well below ground level at the foot of a flight of stairs.

Local people had reminded me that at one time Gaza was a Christian center, the seat of a bishop almost as exalted as the bishop in Alexandria, Egypt. In those ancient days the main church had been what was now the grand mosque and this small church with its cemetery was only a chapel for weddings and funerals.

Alice's mother had died soon after they had returned to Gaza and it was here in the churchyard that she had been buried and where Alice had spent numberless hours grieving. There were no grass or flowers as every available space was filled with tombs and markers.

Now in the midst of this new crisis she had gone instinctively to her mother's grave. "If my mother had lived everything would be different," she said again as she bade me good-bye, turned, and went down the steps and out the front gate. I went back into the house and gathered up the cups we had been drinking from. Im Halid was in the kitchen squatting on the floor before a large tray on which some rice had been spread. Very patiently she was separating the good grains from the small black stones. "Sitt Alice is going to get married in Egypt?" she asked without looking up.

"How did you know?" I asked.

"Nothing is a secret in Gaza."

"Her relatives must be cruel." I said.

"Not cruel," Im Halid said patiently. "It is our way. A woman needs protection."

"But she is a teacher. She is earning her own money. Why can't she manage by herself?"

For a moment Im Halid stopped shifting the rice back and forth and looked up at me and once again patiently replied, "Without a man there are many problems." With that she went back to sorting the rice and would say no more. It was up to me to put together the pieces if I was going to understand what she was trying to tell me.

Perhaps, I thought, *They have found an ounce of prevention to be worth a pound of cure.* I had not thought of Fouziyah for a long time but she was a single woman who came to the hospital from time to time in a desperate state. She had no family and no way of earning a living. In order to keep body and soul together, she was allowed to live in a home where she agreed to be the servant of the wife and mistress of the husband. Relatives of single women always feared for them and I began to see that it was out of a genuine concern.

All the next day I thought about Alice. Finally, as the sun set and the first star appeared, I knew she must be in Cairo. I could imagine her nervousness and fear as she hailed a taxi and ordered the driver to take her to the home of her relatives. I would not know until she returned whether she was to be married or not. If they skipped the engagement party the wedding could be very soon.

I cringed at the thought. Alice loved the church, and she would miss teaching school and visiting in the hospital. She would be frustrated and lonely in Cairo. Even worse, the man knew nothing about Alice. He simply wanted a younger wife and was ready to marry her just from the description her relatives had given him. On the other hand the fact that he was wealthy made him more than acceptable to her relatives. There was no love here, and she could not hope for much understanding.

That night sitting in the small parlor studying my next day's Arabic lesson I kept thinking about Alice. She would be gone for a whole month. There was no telephone connection with Cairo, and I knew she wouldn't write. I would just have to wait until she came back to find out what had happened.

In the meantime I had my hands full getting Philip ready to go to school in Lebanon. It would be very different from the sunny room with its jumble of desks and maps that had been our school-room.

I had no idea whether he would use the paper and already-stamped envelopes I had packed in his suitcase. Even if he wrote, it would take so long for the letters to arrive that any crisis would be over by the time we heard about it.

I knew he was worried. Several times I had found him sitting on his bed in the afternoon, quiet and withdrawn. It was obvious that he was trying to put all the pieces together and to his twelve-year-old mind it didn't seem fair. When I asked him what he was worried about, he shrugged and said he had had a bad dream. In it, the moon had crashed into the sun and everything had gone black.

I was appalled at the imagery expressed in his dream. Of course he was disturbed. To him it was as though his whole world, the only world he knew, was about to vanish. We prayed about it and he felt better, but I went round and round trying to find some better way. It was obvious that scholastically he would be better off in Beirut, but I wondered what would happen to him that year and whether we would look back on this decision and wish we had done something else.

The end of the summer finally came and Philip, along with Bruce Young who was also going to school in Beirut, crowded into the black station wagon with all their luggage and rode the few miles down the main street of Gaza out to the airfield where the U.N. plane was waiting. The whole airstrip with its tiny clapboard customs house seemed no larger than a postage stamp in comparison with any other airfield I had ever seen. However, in spite of its size each bag had to be opened and the contents examined before the boys were free to enjoy their new status as students going off to school.

Many pictures were taken that day and all show two boys holding tennis racquets and smiling. Brothers, sisters, and parents with some nurses who had ridden out in the van can be seen standing in the background. Some pictures show the plane, and one marvels at how very small it actually was, sitting in the tall grass of the field.

There were hugs, kisses, and tears which the camera did not catch, nor did it catch the sinking feeling in the pit of our stomachs as the plane took off and too soon became only a moving dot in the bright blue sky.

I stood looking at the blowing grass, reluctant to get back in the car. This airstrip was so small. Already the shepherd had led his sheep back to graze where just a short time before the plane had left tire marks in the dark soil. I knew that in Beirut the airport was large and complicated. *Surely,* I thought, *the Kings will be there to meet them.*

I felt an arm around my waist. It was Madeline, the student nurse. "Alice is back." she said. "I'm sure she'll be coming by this afternoon to tell us all about her trip."

"Is she married?" I asked.

"I don't know. I just heard from one of the other nurses who rode back on the train with her that she is home."

I crowded into the station wagon and hardly noticed the slow progress as the car inched along between donkeys and camels and women with jars on their heads toward the main street. *If Alice is home she must not have gotten married,* I thought. *How had she managed such a thing? I can hardly wait to hear her story.*

We had barely gotten out of the station wagon when Alice appeared. The usual smile was gone, but there was at the same time a look of satisfaction. She could hardly wait to tell me the news. "I didn't get married," she said as she sank down into the moss green chair in my parlor.

I began asking questions. Had she bought the material for new dresses? Was there an engagement? Had she ever met the man before? How had she escaped? To all these questions Alice was almost indifferent. It seemed enough that she had gotten back to Gaza, and she could not understand why anything else mattered.

"Yes, yes," she said finally. "I did meet him. He was old and a Catholic, not even Greek Orthodox. Thank God I didn't have to marry him. It would have been impossible."

"But how did you manage to get the wedding called off? Did you cry and plead and promise to do anything the family asked if they would just let you out of this marriage?"

Alice didn't answer at first but I could see that it had never occured to her to do any of those things. "I prayed." she said finally. "I just prayed and the wedding was called off, but that doesn't mean I am out of the trouble. My relatives are furious. They blame me for everything."

Alice would say nothing more of the trip to Egypt but I could see that it had been a traumatic experience. In fact it had been so traumatic that she couldn't bring herself to talk about it.

I changed the subject and told her about Philip's leaving and how worried I was. "Don't worry," she said, "everything will be all right. Many blessings are coming, so don't worry."

A month later holding Philip's letter in my hand and with tears blinding my eyes so that I could hardly read, I told Alice how upset Philip had been over the news of the Cuban missle crisis. "There was talk of all Americans being evacuated by the Sixth Fleet and speculation as to what a war with Russia could mean to the Middle East," Philip wrote. "Here at the mission we had many prayer meetings and I was afraid I would never see any of you again."

"I can't stand a whole year of this," I complained to Alice. "Where are the blessings you were telling me about?"

"Be patient," she said. "They are coming. You have no faith, Mrs. Dorr. You have to have faith."

Before I realized it almost four-and-a-half years had passed since we came to Gaza and it was time to go home on our furlough. I was packing and getting ready to leave for the year in Baltimore where David would be working with a research team at Johns Hopkins Medical School.

I was feeling better about Philip. Once the threat of war was over, he had experienced a good year with an excellent teacher. However, there remained some question as to whether we would be able to come back to Gaza.

"Alice," I said as I stood among the suitcases and boxes we were tying to pack, "we may not be able to come back. In another year both Paul and Debby will have to go away to school and we aren't ready to send them off to Beirut. Communication is impossible. We have no idea what is happening from September to Christmas and then from Christmas until the end of the year. Philip writes better than either of them and we got very few letters from him."

For a moment Alice was silent and then, rubbing her hand over the rounded side of my big black trunk, she said, "I'm sure you will be back. I don't know just how things will work out but they will, and you will be back."

I didn't argue because I really wanted to come back, but in my heart I believed there were too many problems and one year at home would not begin to solve them. "We'll see," I said, and went on sorting the clothes that we would need on our trip home.

CHAPTER
9

Much could be written of the year in Baltimore and the letters that flew back and forth discussing the school situation and a new development that would take Dr. Young and his family to Yemen. "If I am to take advantage of the opportunity to start a hospital in Yemen," Jim Young wrote, "we will need you here in Gaza. We have found a school in Alexandria, Egypt that I think will be just right for our children and yours."

With this news we began packing to go back to Gaza. A proper boarding school had been found and we were needed. We bought our tickets on the *Excalibur*, a ship which left New York and toured through the Mediterranean before landing at the harbor in Beirut, Lebanon. It made a stop in Alexandria and we would be able to go out to the school and visit.

Getting off the ship and going to visit the school was more traumatic than I had expected. Suddenly "boarding school," was not just a possibility but a very evident reality. The taxi pulled up in front of the walled enclosure and I read the name *Shutz* on the gatepost. The trees and grassy lawns looked a bit shabby and play worn. It was August, and the swings and swimming pool looked bleak and uninviting. I was not impressed.

The buildings were obviously old and the rooms inside large and uninviting. I felt a growing panic rise within me that I had already made the decision, this was the school my children would have to attend.

Since Debby was the youngest I was most concerned about her. As I stood in the doorway of one of the student rooms I noticed everything. There were no closets only chests of drawers and an oversized, crudely built cupboard for hanging clothes. The windows were large and curtainless. It was summer and I consoled myself with the thought that dormitories always looked bare and ugly under such circumstances.

To my surprise all three children—Philip, Paul, and Debby—liked the school. "Mother," Debby said, "when you talked about going to a boarding school I thought it would be all modern and new. I like this school. There are dogs and cats everywhere and a tree house over by the tennis courts."

We crowded back into the taxi and hurried down to our ship. When we reached Gaza there would be only a month before school opened and I wondered if we would be either psychologically or physically ready to let the children go so soon.

Back in Gaza we found a joyous welcome. U.N. friends dropped by and patients from some of the refugee camps and others from the town itself came to express their happiness at our return, but it was the usual reception on the lawn that made us feel at home. There were big tubs of orange-colored bottled drinks and cookies and everyone from cleaners and cooks to doctors and student nurses sat around under the trees on folding chairs and talked. I looked for Alice, but to my surprise she was nowhere to be seen.

We were to be living in the quaint old cottage beside the tennis court, and there was a great deal of unpacking to be done. Beds were already set up, but sheets had to be found and dishes located. I was going through a box looking for matching single sheets when I noticed someone walking across the porch, and then I saw Alice standing outside the screen door balancing a dish so she could ring the bell.

"Alice," I almost shouted as I dropped everything and hurried to the door.

"I brought you some *baytanjan* for dinner." Alice looked tired and worn but she was smiling.

I took the dish and thanked her. "Where were you this afternoon?" I asked as I set it down.

"I was cooking this," She said, motioning to the casserole. I sensed there was something wrong. Her smile had faded too quickly and she seemed diffident, almost cool.

"Has this been a good year? Are you still teaching?" Alice hadn't written so I knew nothing of what had been happening to her while we had been gone.

"Yes, I'm teaching." She sat on the edge of her chair and nervously ran her finger around the binding on the cushion.

"How is Melia?" I asked in a desperate effort to make conversation.

"Melia? I don't live with them any more."

"What has happened? Where are you living?"

"I lived with a couple in the church for awhile but that didn't work out, and now I am living in one room of a house behind the hospital." She didn't look at me and she spoke in a very controlled, matter-of-fact manner that worried me.

"What happened?"

She shrugged and stood up, "I have had trouble, much trouble. It would take too long to tell."

"But Alice, you must tell me. Maybe I can do something to help."

"No. There is nothing you can do."

"Well maybe if I can't do something perhaps I can get someone else in the church to help."

I noticed her stiffen, "It is someone in the church that has caused most of the problem."

"Someone in the church?" I could hardly believe what I was hearing. While Christians from the Greek Orthodox Church attended all of our meetings the actual membership of our church was very small. "Who was it? What did they do?"

To my surprise Alice stood up and turned to leave. She paused for a moment at the door and for the first time looked at me, "I am going back to the Greek Church." she said. "I have just waited for you to come and tell me it was all right for me to go back." With that she opened the door and was gone.

I went to the door and looked in all directions but couldn't see her anyplace. I closed the screen and tried to put all the pieces together. It was evident that Alice had entered some very difficult time of trial and testing. I intended to find out what had happened and who had caused the problem.

It was harder than I had expected. When I mentioned it to Ed and Anne Nicholas they knew that Alice had not been herself and that she was going through a difficult time with her sister. "Melia is upset first because she became a Baptist and then because she goes around praying for people."

"Do you know of anyone in the church that has caused her a problem?" I asked.

They looked genuinely surprised, "No, of course not. Everyone likes Alice."

Next I asked our Egyptian pastor's wife, "Has Alice had any problems in the church while I was gone?"

She seemed puzzled that I should ask. "No," she said, "Why do you ask?"

Alice came to teach her Sunday School class but didn't stay for church, and I noticed that she didn't come on Wednesday night. This wasn't like Alice. Again, I tried to get to the bottom of the trouble but she wouldn't tell me.

Now I was genuinely concerned. I decided to visit Alice in the rooms she had taken with two old ladies who lived in the warren of houses behind the hospital. I got the key to the back gate from the pharmacy and hurried across the courtyard full of patients to the part of the compound wall that was almost hidden from view by a row of buildings that made up a major part of the wall. The key was always hard to turn in the lock, and I almost wished I could manage to climb over the wall like most of the children did.

Once out in the back streets it was hard to tell one house from another. The street was so narrow that two people could pass comfortably but not big enough for a car. The buildings were ancient and all connected. They rose above me three or four stories with only a door and some upper windows opening onto the street. There were some courtyards, and the house Alice had described was one of these. "I'll leave the door ajar," she had promised.

I found the house just as she had described it. I gave the door a slight nudge. There, sitting under a lemon tree telling stories was Alice. When she saw me she quickly dismissed the children with the promise to tell them more stories later. She smiled and I could see that she was genuinely pleased that I had come. *"Ahlan, ah- lan,"* she said over and over as she moved a wicker chair into the shade and urged me to sit down.

"I have only one room." she explained, "and it's nicer out here."

"But why are you here at all?" I asked, trying to get right to the heart of the matter that bothered me.

"It is quite simple. Melia won't let me come home as long as I am a Baptist."

"And. . . ." I said, knowing this was not the whole story.

"Well, in our Baptist church it seems they have so many young girls to do the teaching that they don't really need me."

"And. . . ."

"Well, the Greek priest has wanted me to come and be in charge of the Sunday School they are going to start"

"Can't you teach in both? I'm sure you will be needed."

"They meet at the same time so I will have to choose."

I could see that while she was answering my questions she was not willing to discuss them. I was convinced that there was more to the trouble than what she was telling me. "I can see that you have problems but they don't seem to be any bigger than those you have faced in the past. Yet, you are obviously very upset and unhappy."

I could tell by the quick look she darted in my direction that I had hit some sore point. "I must get you something to drink." she said trying to dismiss the subject.

She went to the house and came out with a tray that had obviously been carefully prepared earlier. She set it down on a small wicker table and uncorked the vacuum bottle and poured out the warm, sweet tea into a cup and handed it to me. This was a signal that she wanted no more questions, so I changed the subject and told her about our year in Baltimore.

Only when I stood to leave did I again mention the problem.

"Alice," I said, "who is the person in our church who has caused you such trouble that you don't want to come anymore?"

Again I could tell by the quick intake of breath and startled look that I had hit upon some deep-seated problem.

"I can't tell."

"Then tell me what happened. What did this person do?"

"She told people that I was a foolish woman and I had made a big mistake leaving the Greek Church and becoming a Baptist."

I could tell by the way she told me that there was something in the situation that had hurt her deeply and yet on the surface it wasn't evident. Alice had endured joyfully when many worse things were being said about her. "Did she also say that no one in the Baptist church or at the hospital really liked you? Did she maybe say they made fun of you?"

I could tell by the way she turned her head away to hide the hurt that it was something like this that had so upset her.

"I'm going to go back to the Greek Church." she said finally. "I was just waiting for you to come back."

"If you would just tell me who has been saying these awful things. They aren't true. Who in the church would do such a thing?"

Again she shook her head, "I can't tell you. It's true, but I can't tell you. I just want you to say I can go back."

This was the beginning of a very peculiar situation. Every time I saw Alice she would ask me only one question. "Mrs. Dorr, please say I can go back to the Greek Church."

The climax finally came when I was on the third floor of the hospital having tea with some of the nurses. The doorbell rang and Ali, the cook, called me out of the room. "It's Alice," Ali said. "She says it's important. She has to see you."

Alice was at the door looking pale and worn with none of her usual bright happiness. "I'm just having tea. Can you come in and have a cup with us?" I asked.

"No, no," she said. "I don't want anything. Just tell me I can go."

"Go?" I said, temporarily forgetting the other encounters.

"Yes, tell me I can go back to the Greek Church." She wasn't joking. She was dead serious and I wondered why she wanted this from me.

"Alice, I'm not the one to tell you what to do. You have to pray about it."

"No, no," she said, "I don't want to pray about it."

"But, you always pray about everything. How is this different?"

"I have already picked out a sign. If it happens I'll know I am to go back.

"A sign?" I questioned. "What kind of a sign?"

"I told God that if you said 'go back' then I would go back but I wouldn't go back unless you said those words."

"Alice," I said, "Come back over to my house. We have to talk about this. I'm not the one to tell you what to do."

We walked over to the house without saying a word as I pondered the whole problem. I didn't see that it would hurt for Alice to go teach in the Greek Orthodox Sunday School, but it shouldn't be decided in such a way, nor should she be going because she was in trouble with this mysterious person in the church who gossiped about her.

I approached the problem from every angle but still Alice wouldn't tell me who the person was that had caused her so much trouble nor would she admit that her test wasn't a valid one. Finally I said, "Alice, it's all right for you to go back to the Greek Church on one condition. You must promise me that you will pray about it and do whatever the Lord shows you to do."

"But Mrs. Dorr," she said, "I don't want to know what God wants me to do. What if he tells me to stay?"

Once again I saw how devastating this situation had been but I dared not relent. She who had trusted God so implicitly for others had to trust Him in this too or she would no longer be a channel for God's help to others. "It is not easy, but if he tells you to stay he will also straighten out the problem so it won't be so hard. Promise me, Alice," I said. "Promise me you will pray about it."

She was silent for a long time and then without another word she turned and walked down the steps. I noticed that all the bounce had gone out of her step and her shoulders sagged until I would not have recognized her as the same woman I had known and loved.

I wondered what she would do. Suddenly the miracles of answered prayer for patients seemed easy compared with this. When one wanted out so badly, was it possible to hear the voice of the Lord? I wondered what would happen to her. I had so easily promised that the Lord would work everything out if he asked her to stay.

Wouldn't it be more likely for Alice to reason that a whole year had gone by and there had been no help? Everything had only gotten worse. How could she trust God to help her now? Wasn't it more logical to just use her own wits and do the safe thing?

As I got into bed that night, I mentally steeled myself for Alice's answer. There was no doubt that she would go. It would take some sort of a miracle to change this downward spiral. I hated to have her go feeling so unloved and unappreciated. Again I tried to think of who could have hurt her so much and I could think of no one.

CHAPTER
10

A week went by and I neither saw Alice nor heard anything about her. No one had seen her. I began to be concerned and then alarmed. It was a Friday, and I had been awake since 5:00 AM when the earliest call to prayer cut through the darkness like a dull sword. David got up and hurried off to make rounds at the hospital, and eventually the sun shone through the closed blinds making bright patterns on the tile floor. I could hear children's voices as they rose and fell in a happy blend and then, finally, the chapel bell with its clear clanging that seemed to belie the heavy foreboding that I felt.

For the hundredth time I went over the advice I had given Alice and wondered if I had been right. It would certainly solve her problems with Melia and her friends if she went back to the Greek Church.

I opened the blinds and looked out to see where the children had gone. There was no one in sight. The courtyard was empty. I immediately thought of the pepper trees. The children liked to climb the big pepper trees on the far side of the tennis court or swing on the large homemade swings. Just in time, I remembered that their favorite pastime was to climb the wall in the far corner where climbing was made easy by the indented footholds that must have been as old as the wall itself. Once balanced at the top of the wall, they could look down on the main street and see the kaleidoscope of people, animals, and cars.

Most interesting of all was a crudely built ice-cream stand directly beneath the wall, and the children had found that for a few piasters the friendly owner would hand up an assortment of blue, purple, or yellow cones of the icy mixture.

"*Boozah, boozah.*" Paul and John shouted the Arabic word for ice cream as they hung perilously over the wall; their feet barely holding in the niches while Debby and Carol Beth waited patiently near the bed of bright calendulas for their share.

"No ice cream until you have eaten your breakfast." I said, as I hurried through the dew-ladened grass to help the boys down. We marched single file back across the tennis court and through the small door that led into our courtyard, all the while the boys complaining and the little girls crying that they had missed their treat.

"You know better than to eat anything before breakfast and besides, I'm not sure the ice cream is good for you."

"We never have gotten sick," they chorused.

It was true. The children never seemed to get sick no matter what they ate; however, I could picture in my mind tuberculosis and all sorts of terrible diseases from eating ice cream made with unpasteurized milk.

David had been at the hospital making rounds. He would then be in chapel until it was time for surgery, so he could not eat breakfast with the family. Breakfast consisted of whatever could be bought in the market, usually fresh fruit, vegetables in season, and U.N. rations that somehow leaked out for general consumption. Most often these rations were something the refugees didn't like such as very salty canned bacon, canned oatmeal, and now there had appeared rather mysteriously big boxes of corn flakes. Most of the time we ate the local produce.

We had just seated ourselves at the table when the front door bell rang and Hassan announced that Alice wanted to see me. My heart sank. I was sure she had come to tell me she was leaving the church. I pushed back my chair and hurried to the door. Alice never came this early but it was Friday and there was no school. I was surprised to see her standing behind the screen smiling with the same radiant smile she used to have before the trouble began. Whatever the outcome it was wonderful to see her so happy again.

"Something special has happened," I observed as I opened the door and invited her in. "It is evident that you have had good news."

"Not so much good news as an answer. I'm not going back to the Greek Church."

For a moment she enjoyed the surprise I must have exhibited. I had expected any response but that. "What happened?" I asked. "What could possibly have happened to make such a change?"

"It's a strange story even for me," she said. "I can hardly believe it myself, but there is no doubt about what I am to do."

I glanced into the dining room and saw that the children were already eating their corn flakes and loading their round slices of bread with the new fig jam I had made. There was time to talk, so I motioned for Alice to sit in the moss green chair she usually chose and I curled up on the sofa eager to hear what had happened. Whatever it was, I knew it must be something unusually convincing to change Alice's mind so suddenly.

"The other day when I went home," she began, "I didn't want to pray about it, but I knew you were right. I cooked my food and ate, then straightened my room. I did everything I could think of to forget what I knew I should do. Finally, when it was time to go to bed, I knelt and prayed that God would show me what to do. 'If you will show me what I should do,' I prayed, 'then I promise that I will do it, even if it is difficult.'

"I went to bed and almost immediately I had a vision of the Lord standing before me and telling me, 'I have chosen you,' he said. 'I need you. Separate from the first church and go to the second.' This happened three times, and then I woke up. It seemed so real. His voice was strong and firm, like thunder. The words were so distinct I couldn't misunderstand.

"I sat up in bed and lit my lamp. I looked around my room and saw that nothing had changed. I began to doubt what I had seen and heard. *How could I have seen the Lord so plainly in this room,* I wondered. *How could I have heard him so clearly?*

"I began to think that this was not the Lord's voice at all. I knew that Satan is the great deceiver and can change himself into many forms. I reached for my Bible and decided that if I opened it to a verse that gave me some direction I would trust the verse rather than the voice. I opened my Bible to the chapter that tells of Peter's vision in Joppa and how in the vision he was led to believe he should go witness to the Gentile, Cornelius. I saw the word *go*, and as I looked at it the word seemed to be meant just for me. I closed the Bible and put it on my bedside table.

" 'Thank you, Lord,' Now I know this is right and I am to go back to the Greek Church. I deliberately put the vision away and lay down to sleep convinced that I should go back to the Greek Orthodox Church. Of course, that was what I wanted to do. It would solve all my problems. I wouldn't have to see the person who had hurt me so badly and I would be pleasing Melia and her friends.

"Right away I drifted off to sleep and then a very strange thing happened. I again had a vision, or a dream; I don't know which, but it was very real. It is still very real as though it were something that actually happened.

"I was on the drive that comes into the hospital and passes the church. It was dark, and I noticed that there was a service going on in the church. The lights in the church were very bright and I could hear singing. I walked faster, as I didn't want anyone to see me, but just as I came to the church a woman came out and invited me to come in.

"Impatiently I insisted that I was in a hurry and couldn't stop. I saw her turn and go back into the church just as I started down some steps that seemed strangely like the steps that led down into the Greek Orthodox Church. As I went down dark spots began to appear on my arms and my clothes. I tried to brush them off but as soon as I brushed off one it would reappear in another place.

"I looked around and it seemed that I was in a dark tunnel, but in the distance I could still hear, very faintly, the singing from the church. Suddenly, blocking the way, I saw some large soldiers. 'Alice Antone,' one of them said, 'go to that meeting in the church you just left. Those who go will be blessed.'

" 'Who are you and how did you know my name?' I asked, though some inner instinct told me that they were angels.

" 'We are angels sent to guard that small church,' one of them said as he pointed through the tunnel toward the church. 'We have been stationed here night and day so that no evil thing can harm them.'

"As I looked back toward the way I had come I could still see the church. Its lights were bright spots in the darkness and the singing was now joyful and insistent. In a great fright, I turned and ran up the steps and as I ran the spots disappeared.

"That is all I remember. It was so vivid and so real it didn't seem like a dream, but once again in the morning I dismissed it as a regular dream that had no meaning for me. You see, I didn't want to believe that God was answering my prayer and telling me to do something that I didn't want to do. However, it was real enough so that the next Sunday I didn't go to the Greek Church, nor did I come to the Baptist church. I stayed home.

"No one from the Baptist church came to see me, but the wife of the Greek priest came to visit and I promised that the next Sunday I would go to the Greek Church.

"That night it happened again. Jesus appeared in my room and this time I knew it was not just a dream. 'Don't be afraid,' he said. 'I am God speaking with you. I have spoken with you before. I want you and I need you, but you must separate from the first church and stay with the second.' Three times he said, 'I want you and I need you. If you return to the old church I will judge you.'

"This time I knew it was the Lord's voice and I fell down at his feet and said, 'I am ready. I know you have answered my prayer and I will do what you want me to do.'

"That was just last night that I saw him and I knew that it was Jesus speaking with me. I can't go back now." Alice daubed at her face with her handkerchief.

I was deeply moved because I knew what a struggle it must have been. She had wanted to do the easy thing. She had been so disillusioned and hurt by someone in our church she wanted above all else to get away from them. She also wanted desperately to have peace with her family and the approval again of her friends and the community. This was more than just a dream or a figment of her subconscious, and yet questions began to rise. "Was this a dream?" I asked finally.

"It may have been a dream, but it was as real as my sitting here and talking with you."

"You heard a voice?" I couldn't resist asking all the questions that were now clamoring for answers.

"It was as though, . . ." Alice hesitated as she struggled to describe it accurately. "It was as though he was behind a glass and I could see his lips move but I heard the words in my heart."

"And you are not going back to the Greek Church now?"

"Of course not. I can't." For a moment the old cloud seemed to darken her face. "I know it was the voice of God and I can't go against that. That's why I didn't want to pray. I wanted you to tell me to go."

"Would you have been satisfied with that?"

She shrugged, "I suppose not, but it would have been so much easier."

"Can you tell me now who it is in the church that has caused you so much trouble?"

She looked startled and then stood up abruptly, "No, no, I can't tell."

"But we must get this straightened out."

"I can't; I don't want to. It's asking too much."

"But how can you come back to church?"

"I won't go to the Greek Church," she said very slowly, "but neither will I come anyplace where that woman is."

"Will you pray about it?"

Her face paled and she shook her head, "No, no, I won't pray about this. It is asking too much."

She walked to the door and I could tell that she was very upset. She didn't say any more and I knew it was useless to pursue the question further. I was afraid that she had come this far on a very difficult pilgrimage and would be able to go no further. Forgiveness is never easy for anyone, but I had found that for my Arab friends it was the very hardest thing to do.

Once again I tried to figure out who the person could be that had gossiped about her. I now knew it was a woman, but beyond that I had no idea who it could be. In spite of a supernatural intervention that had brought her back to the church she was still a long way from any real feeling of belonging. I ached for her and wondered what would happen next. Would she drift away or could she overcome this most difficult challenge?

CHAPTER
11

The month passed in a flurry of getting Philip, Paul, and Debbie ready to leave for boarding school in Alexandria, Egypt. To reach the school there would be a full day's trip down across the Sinai to the canal and then to Cairo and finally through the flat delta region to Alexandria. Anything forgotten would have to wait for their return at Christmastime.

There was considerable consolation in the knowledge that three of the Young's children, Bruce, Mark, and Kay as well as Eddie Nicholas were going, too. Our children would at least be entering this strange new world with some of their best friends.

When the time to leave finally came we crowded into the black station wagon at the unlikely hour of 3 AM and headed toward the southern border of the Gaza Strip. It was necessary to start early because there were checkpoints where passports were stamped and sometimes even the luggage checked, then there was always a big pileup of cars at the Suez Canal. There were only certain times between ships that the ferry was running and it was important to be near the head of the line.

We had been to Egypt only once or twice before as it involved such a complicated procedure of getting a permit to leave Gaza and then a visa to enter Egypt, as well as finding a convenient time to leave the hospital. "Does everyone have their passports? Have you forgotten anything? Remember it will be Christmas before you get home again." David was especially concerned about passports as the whole trip could come to an end at the first checkpoint if anyone was without their passport.

As the car sped through the darkness we looked out the windows at the small village of Raffa and then the palms of Deir Bella, and later we had the never-to-be-forgotten sight of the sun like a great round ball coming up over the rolling sand dunes. All the time the road stretched before us like a measuring tape running between drifts of blowing sand and barren dunes peppered with small, twisted shrubs.

By the time we reached the canal the sun was high in the sky. We pulled up and parked at the end of a growing line of pickups and Mercedes. They were waiting for the first ships to pass so they could cross on the ferry.

"Look, look, Dad. That big ship is floating right on top of the sand." Philip was the first to catch sight of the seeming marvel. We looked in the direction he was pointing and there on the horizon was a ship that appeared to be sailing directly toward us over the sand dunes. No matter how often we drove to Egypt we never failed to be impressed with this phenomenon.

When the ship had passed we were able to move onto the ferry and cross the narrow body of water that made up the canal. On the other side stood the customs officials motioning for us to unload all of our luggage and bring it inside the shelter for inspection. Everything was examined. Nothing was overlooked, and it was late afternoon before we were able to pack things back in the suitcases and hurry on our way to Cairo and Alexandria.

The wait at the canal and the long time spent in the customs shed made us miss dinner at the school. "We can find something for the children to eat," one of the teachers explained, "but you will have to find a restaurant on your way to Mrs. Dumriecher's house where you will be staying."

All this was so new to us. We helped carry the suitcases to their rooms and said a hurried good-bye as the children were led away by one of the teachers.

We were tired and it was late. We decided to go straight to Mrs. Dumriecher's house. We found it behind a high wall on a very narrow street. When we knocked on the big metal gate it was opened by an old man wearing the traditional turban and *galabia* of the Egyptian servant. He broke into a smile of welcome. "My name's Mohammed," he said with a heavy accent. "Mrs. Dumriecher is not here, but she has everything ready."

He took our suitcases and pointed with his lantern to the cobblestone path that led to a wide, dimly lit veranda. On each side of the path we were vaguely aware of what appeared to be banks and plots of lovely flowers. The sweet smell of tuberoses filled the air. The veranda turned out to be a homey place with wicker chairs and a low table strewn with reading material and crowned with a sewing basket.

The room where we were to sleep had two cots neatly made and a grass mat on the floor. The pillowcases were embroidered and the towels were laid out at the end of the cots. "The bathroom is down the hall," Mohammed said with a flourish of the lantern toward the dark end of the long hall and then added, "the electricity is off. I'll have to bring you a lamp."

We sat on the cots in total darkness and wondered about the children. Were they in bed yet? Were they frightened or homesick? Everything had happened so fast. We hadn't expected it to be like this. Actually we hadn't known what to expect.

Promptly Mohammed was back with the lamp. He set it down on the table and closed the door. We watched as the small lamp cast weird shadows on the high ceiling and walls and listened to the shuffling sound as he went down the hall. Minutes later we heard him clearing his throat as he headed down the path to the front gate.

"Well," I said, opening the basket in which we had carried food for the trip, "We have some bread and some jelly but no knife, only a spoon and I'm starved." I divided the bread and we shared the spoon but we found we were more tired than hungry and were ready to go to bed.

The next morning was as bright as the night before had been dreary. Mrs. Dumriecher proved to be a wonderful hostess. She had a lovely breakfast planned for us at a table beneath a trellis of gorgeous roses. From the table we could look out and see the flowers that we had only sensed the night before. The whole area was within a wall, and the trees and flowers seemed to blossom and thrive like those in the pictures of English gardens that were so popular a generation ago.

Mrs. Dumriecher talked at great length about the wonders of Shultz and its dedicated teachers until we felt much better about leaving the children. Indeed when we finished breakfast and drove back to the school, the children were so busy making new friends we had a hard time getting them aside to give last-minute instructions and to say good-bye. "I don't know what I expected," I said as we drove off, "but it certainly wasn't this. Can you imagine? They aren't even crying!"

"It certainly makes it easier to see them so happy." David said. "I hope everything works out. It won't be perfect, but at least it seems like a really good school."

Back in Gaza the house felt empty and almost deserted with only John and Jimmy left at home. They would be going to a United Nations School down by the beach. It was a unique school just started by the United Nations for its foreign personnel. Each class had only five or six students. No two were from the same country, and it was a problem to decide which country's curriculum would be followed. It was finally decided that the curriculum would be based on the British system and that the children would wear uniforms in U. N. colors made by tailors on the main street of Gaza. The mothers were given small circular, U.N. emblems with instructions to sew them on the pockets of the shirts.

All of this had taken so much of my attention and time that I had not talked to Alice. I had noticed that she wasn't at church or at the women's meetings but she did come late on Wednesday nights and sat in the back and left early. It seemed that she didn't want to talk to anyone and the old joy was gone.

"Alice," I said finally one night when she was the last to leave, "I think it is important for you to tell me who this person is that has hurt you so badly."

For a moment I thought she was going to walk away without

answering, but to my surprise she looked at me and shifted her Bible from one hand to the other as though she wanted to say something. "What good would it do?" She said finally.

"Perhaps together we could think of some way to set things straight."

"That's the trouble," she said no longer looking me in the eye, "I don't want to set things straight. I don't want to see her. I don't want to be where she is."

"But Alice," I said. "This is not hurting her, it is hurting you. You have lost all the joy and you aren't praying for people any more. Maybe if you could just tell me who it is, that would be the first step toward getting rid of your hurt."

"You'll make me go to her and. . . ."

"No, I promise. I won't tell anyone and I won't tell you what to do. That is something you will have to settle yourself."

"It is so hard."

"I know it is hard but you must start someplace for healing to begin."

She looked at me doubtfully, "I'll have to think about it." she said.

"Not pray about it?"

"No, no, I can't pray about it."

With that she left and again I wondered what she would do. I could see this was far harder for her than I had even imagined.

Two days went by and I didn't see Alice at all, then suddenly she appeared beside me as I sat in a chair on the patio studying for my Arabic lesson. I had the tape recorder on and was trying to memorize a new verb. "Arabic is so hard," I said as I switched off the tape and pushed out a chair for her to sit down.

"I can't stay," she said as I offered her a cup of Arabic coffee. "I've decided you're right. I have come to tell you the name."

"Is it someone I am very close to?" I asked, thinking this could be her problem.

"She is someone you see."

"She can't be one of the nurses from Lebanon or Egypt because they don't visit local people that much.

"No, no, I can see that you will suspect everyone if I don't tell you. You see she hurt me so much because I thought she was my friend. It hurts more to find a friend is laughing at you. Then to find she would go visiting and make fun of something I take very seriously has been too hard."

As she spoke I began to see that it could be only one person. "It must be Sitt Hudda," I said. "She is blind but someone is always taking her visiting. I can't imagine her saying cruel things about you though."

"How did you know?" Alice was both surprised and relieved that I had been the one to say the name. "She thinks I was stupid to be baptized when I have already been baptized as a baby in the Greek Church, and she tells everyone that I must be simpleminded to leave the Greek Church."

"But she has become a Baptist."

"She says it is necessary for her if she is going to work in the hospital with Baptists."

"Why were you baptized again?" Alice had made the decision before I came to Gaza and I had never discussed it with her.

"Ever since I've been reading my Bible I have known that it was important for me to be baptized by my own decision. As a baby it was my parent's decision.

"So that is the problem with Sitt Hudda."

"She also thinks I am foolish to go around praying for people when it upsets Melia."

"And . . . why don't you stop?"

Alice looked startled until she realized I was not being critical. "I pray for people because I know God can heal them and I am sorry for them."

For awhile we sat and neither one said anything. I had really been surprised to find it was Sitt Hudda, but the more I thought about it the more the pieces fit. Sitt Hudda had come with the hospital. When the British left Palestine the C.M.S. Mission left also and they asked Southern Baptists to take over the hospital on the Gaza Strip. Sitt Hudda was blind but had found a useful place as a general visitor among the patients and a storyteller to the children. She spent a great deal of time visiting in the Christian homes of people who lived around the Greek Church behind the hospital.

"Why would Sitt Hudda say these things? Didn't she know it would cause you trouble?"

"I don't know why she did it."

"Could she have been jealous?"

"I don't know. All I know is that I can't stand to be in the same room with her. It makes me feel sick."

"I understand," I said, "but I wish you would pray about it."

Alice stood up and reached for her bag of schoolbooks. "I don't want to think about it anymore. It has spoiled everything."

I watched her leave and wished I could help her. There had been some reluctance to use Alice in the Sunday School as much as before, but I could not tell whether it was from the influence of Sitt Hudda or caused by Alice's own attitude. She no longer smiled or attended meetings regularly and this could have caused some of her trouble.

I had no way of telling what Sitt Hudda's motives were, but I was fairly sure that short of some miracle Alice would not be able to forgive her. If she couldn't forgive her, Alice's unique ministry might be over. Whether she went back to the Greek Church or stayed in the Baptist church would make no difference. As long as she felt so strongly about Sitt Hudda there would be a dark cloud over everything she did.

Time passed quickly and before we knew it Christmas was approaching. It was while we were preparing for the Christmas program and decorating the church with the poinsettias that blossomed so abundantly at that time of year that Alice suddenly appeared. I could tell by the look on her face that something special had happened.

"I am not angry at Sitt Hudda anymore," she whispered.

"What happened?" I was amazed at such a change.

"I knew I would have to forgive Sitt Hudda. Last night I prayed, and then finally this morning I told God that I would come here to the hospital and he would have to do the rest. I was willing but I didn't know how to go about it.

"You came this morning?

"No, I came just an hour ago, at dinner time. I spent the whole day getting up courage just to come to the hospital."

"You went to Sitt Hudda's room. . .?" I tried to encourage her.

"I wouldn't have imagined I could go to her room but something quite unexpected happened. God answered my prayer."

"You thought it was easier for him to heal someone than to change an attitude?"

"Yes, yes. It seemed impossible."

"Then, how did it happen?" I was getting impatient to hear the story.

"I was walking by the dining hall and turned the corner to go in when, suddenly, there in front of me was Sitt Hudda. She was leaning on Madeline's arm and walking slowly. Evidently she had come down for dinner. Madeline said hello to me, but I didn't answer because I didn't want Sitt Hudda to know I was there. To my surprise she turned to me and said. 'Dear, I have forgotten my shawl and it is cold. Could you run to my room and get it for me?'

"Did she know it was you?"

"No, she just realized someone was standing there, and she took for granted it was another student nurse. Without a word I went to her room. It was difficult but not as difficult as if she had been there. I found her shawl lying on the bed and very quickly started back to the dining hall. On the way I realized that just by going to her room and getting her shawl I had been able to break through a barrier.

"I went into the dining hall and gave her the shawl. I spoke to her and she seemed really glad to hear my voice."

"Did you say anything to her about the trouble you have had because of her talking?"

"No, I had intended to but I realized I would only be digging up old bones. I could see that she felt no resentment toward me and I knew that my anger toward her was gone. It was a miracle.

God had removed all the bitterness, and I didn't want it to come back."

Late that night I was sitting at my typewriter in the little room across the patio. I had been writing an article for one of the Baptist papers and had worked hard on the last line. I pulled the papers out of the machine and began to check for mistakes in spelling. To my surprise my mind kept returning to all that had happened to Alice that day. It seemed such a simple thing. To go to Sitt Hudda's room and get her shawl was not at all complicated but it would have been impossible a week or even a day before. It was evident that Alice had to first be willing and then God was faithful to open a way for her to act out the forgiveness she was already feeling.

I wondered if she would start praying for people again. It had been a long time since Alice had started on this downward spiral. "You can tell when a person is right with God," someone has said, "because the Holy Spirit starts working in their life again."

In the next few months there seemed to be no sudden change. Alice came and went rather quietly but smiling and happy. She no longer avoided Sitt Hudda and she was once again ready to participate in every aspect of the church. Only in the spring, when school was out did anything unusual happen and then only because she was again going to Egypt for her summer vacation.

CHAPTER
12

"Tomorrow school will be out and I will have to decide whether I am going to Egypt to visit my relatives this year." Alice had lingered after the singspiration in the nurses' sitting room.

"Do you really have any choice?"

"Not really but, . . ."

"Could you write and say you are too busy or you need the rest."

"Too busy for relatives? They would be very upset if I wrote that, and if I said I were too tired they would insist I come to them to rest. That is the way of relatives in the Middle East."

It had been several years since Alice had experienced a happy visit with her relatives, and it all seemed to have originated with Alice's baptism and ministry of praying for people. She had worked hard and needed her vacation and I hated to see her go into such a frustrating situation.

As it turned out, when the time came to leave her whole outlook had changed. She was no longer apprehensive. "I saw Jesus," she told me. "It was just like the last time. He seemed to be behind a thick glass. I could see his lips move but heard the words only in my heart. He told me not to be afraid. He would give me the words to say at the right time."

There was no time to question her. She was in a hurry to get home and finish her packing. "I just wanted to tell you," she said, "so you wouldn't worry."

I did worry, however, the whole time she was gone. Alice hadn't changed, and I knew her relatives would not be able to approve of what she was doing. However, when Alice returned at the end of the summer she reprimanded me soundly. "Mrs. Dorr, you have no faith," she said. "How could you worry after Jesus appeared and told me not to be afraid?"

"I know, I know," I confessed and then eagerly asked, "what did happen? Was it different from before?"

"You can't imagine," Alice said sinking into her favorite chair in my little sitting room. "From the first day it was different."

"How was it different? What happened?"

"It's a long story. So much happened I don't even know where to begin."

"Just start at the beginning. I want to hear everything." I was afraid Alice would decide it was too late or have something more important to do. As it turned out she had stayed on purpose to tell me about her summer.

"From the very start things worked out, and before I left all my relatives were proud of me. People were sending taxies to take me to their homes to pray for their relatives. When I left, their priest, the Greek priest, said, "Those Baptists will persecute you, but we would make you a saint."

"How amazing! What made the difference?"

"When I got to Cairo this time I called the whole family together. 'Look," I said, 'You are all angry with me because I was baptized and go around praying for people. Do you think I like having everyone angry? No, of course not. When you know why I have done this then you will understand. It wasn't some idea of mine but it was because Jesus himself appeared to me in several visions and told me what I was to do.

"I then told them all about the vision in Jerusalem and everything that had happened to me since. They were surprised and some of them had tears in their eyes. 'We won't stop you any more,' they said, 'and please pray for us.'

"That's how it began. I prayed for each of them, and they went out and told their friends, and before I knew it people were coming night and day asking me to come pray."

With that she began to tell me the wonderful happenings. Whole families were reunited, people repented, and miraculous cures were not uncommon. Finally I put out my hand and stopped her, "Alice," I said, "was everyone you prayed for healed? Weren't any of your prayers unanswered?"

She stopped and thought. "I don't know what you would call unanswered." There were three that didn't turn out the way I thought they should but the prayers were answered."

"Can you tell me about them?"

"Of course, but why do you always want to know about the difficulties and the problems?"

I was a bit taken aback as I hadn't realized that it would seem this way to Alice. It was true that I listened rather matter-of-factly to wonderful stories of instant healings, but it was the snags that opened up new understanding. "I want to hear everything," I said finally, "but you have to understand that it is the difficult cases that most of us can identify with."

Alice seemed to accept this explanation and proceeded to tell me what had happened. "The first woman had been lying in bed helpless for ten years," Alice said. "When the relatives came to get me in the taxi, they told me they didn't have much hope of a cure but they wanted me to come and pray anyway.

"They took me to her room and I saw a middle-aged woman lying in bed, completely helpless. The shutters were drawn and the room smelled of strong medicine. I told them to open the shutters so I could see the woman more clearly. 'Do you want to be healed?' I asked.

" 'Yes, yes, I want to be healed more than anything in the world. I'm tired of this bed and tired of being dependent on others.' There were tears in her eyes and I told her, 'I have no power to heal but Jesus does, and I will pray for you in Jesus' name and we will see what happens.'

"I began to pray for her, but there was a strange heaviness and I knew she was not going to be healed. As I prayed I saw that the heaviness was resentment and that as long as she held onto the resentment she could not be healed. I removed my hand and opened my eyes to look at her. As I prayed, I said, 'I saw that you have resentment in your heart and as long as that resentment is there you will never get out of this bed.' "

I was shocked at Alice's statement. Though I knew that psychological problems could lead to serious illness, I was amazed that Alice was able to pinpoint the block as resentment. "How did you know the woman had a problem with resentment?" I asked.

Alice didn't answer for a moment. As usual, she hadn't analyzed the situation at all. "I just knew," she said finally. "As I prayed the answer came that she could not be healed because of her resentment."

"So she wasn't healed?"

"No, no, she was healed but she was healed of the resentment first."

Again I was puzzled. If her problem was resentment and she had obviously been afflicted with it for ten years I wondered how she could be healed without months of psychotherapy? "Alice," I asked, "what did you do?"

"The woman began to cry as soon as I mentioned resentment. 'It's my mother-in-law,' she said. 'I hate her and, you are right, I resent her but I can't change.'

"I picked up my purse and started to go. 'Then,' I said, 'you would rather keep your resentment and stay in bed than be healed?'

"She struggled to pull herself up on one elbow so she could reach out to me. 'Don't go. Don't go. Just pray for me that I may be healed.'

" 'It's finished,' I said. 'It's no use. As long as you keep the resentment you will lie in this bed.' Again, I started to go.

" 'No, no, don't go. I want to get rid of the resentment but I can't. I've tried and I can't.'

" 'Would you be willing to let Jesus take the resentment away?'

" 'He can do that?' the woman asked.

" 'Yes, He can if you are willing to release it and sincerely want it to go.'

" 'But what about my mother-in-law? She has done so many terrible things. Who will confront her and punish her. . . .'

" 'You will have to leave that in the Lord's hands. You can only deal with your own heart and life.' I could see that a great struggle was going on inside the woman.

" 'But what if I give it up today and it comes back tomorrow?'

" 'Then you will most likely be back in bed.'

" 'It will come back. I know it will. This is all hopeless.' She began to cry and I felt sorry for her.

" 'Of course it will try to come back, and you will have to give it to Jesus every time. If you persist it will gradually get weaker and finally go. Can you do that?'

" 'Yes, yes, I want it to go. Please pray that it will go.'

"We prayed together for healing of each area in which the resentment had a stronghold, then when we finished I asked two of her brothers to come over to the bed. 'She is weak from lying in bed so long,' I said. 'You will have to help her up. Today you will help her take ten steps, tomorrow fifteen, and the next day twenty, then she will be able to do it herself.'

"And," I asked, "was she really able to get out of bed?"

"Of course. She called before I left to thank me. She had done just as I told her and she was now eating with the family, managing her own bath, and had begun to help in the kitchen."

We sat for awhile each thinking our own thoughts. Alice's story of a failure had turned out to be a great success. I wondered how long it would have taken a psychiatrist to bring about the same results. I also wondered how many times our prayers aren't answered because we are praying for the wrong things. It was evident that without dealing with the resentment Alice could have prayed for years and the woman would not have been healed.

"And what was the next failure?" I asked, looking at my watch to be sure there would be enough time to hear the whole story.

"It was a failure in the daughter's eyes because she asked me to come pray that her mother might be healed but her mother died. However, it wasn't really a failure unless you consider only a return to health success.

"It was the daughter who first contacted me. She told me her mother had suffered from a stroke but she believed she could be healed if I would only come and pray for her. I got ready as soon as possible and went with the messenger to the home of the patient.

"There were some friends and relatives present, and when I entered the room they all made way for me to go straight to the bed. It was obvious the woman had had a stroke, but she was in no pain and seemed to be feeling well. I told her as I always tell every person that I had no power to heal. I simply do as the Bible instructs and ask in Jesus' name. That seemed to please the woman, so I put my hand on her as I always do and began to pray. To my surprise, as I prayed I found a message forming for the woman, 'I love you. I am Jesus. I am waiting for you. A glorious crown is waiting for you because you have done well.'

"The daughter was obviously disappointed but her mother was radiantly happy. I could see that I had brought her the peace and assurance she needed at that moment. She reached out and held my hand, 'Come back tomorrow,' she said. 'Please promise me you'll come back tomorrow.'

"I promised and left. The next day at about the same time I returned to the house with a friend. As we went up the dark stairs to her apartment I suddenly stopped. 'She is dying,' I said, 'When we get there we will find she is either dying or dead.'

"We found the room crowded and as we entered people began to weep and wail. 'She has just died.' I said to my friend.

"The daughter rushed over to me, 'Why did she die? You prayed for her and she died anyway.' At that everyone turned to me and began asking questions through their tears. 'Why did she die? Why wasn't she healed? You prayed for her just yesterday. Why wasn't she healed?'

"I raised my hands and ordered them to be quiet. 'Don't weep for her. Right now she is entering into her reward. There is celebration and rejoicing. Jesus loves her and has come himself to welcome her.'

"At that the mood changed. The people became quiet and one by one they approached the bed with awe as they remembered what I had told her the day before. Only the daughter remained sullen and unhappy. In fact, it was the dead woman's daughter that is the subject of my third failure. Here also it was not really a failure but the wrong diagnosis.

" 'You need to pray for her,' some of the women said as they nodded toward the daughter. 'She is possessed by evil spirits. She often acts strange and her mother was worried about her.' I had noticed this myself, and so before it was time for me to go I asked everyone to leave the room while I talked with the daughter privately. As soon as the women were gone, the daughter asked me to pray for her. We sat down and I began to pray, but as I prayed I found she wasn't demon possessed at all. Instead the word *repent* kept coming. I told her and she began to cry.

" 'What have you been doing?' I asked. 'Why do you need to repent?

"It was as though a dam burst and the words tumbled out in confusion. 'I prayed for children and God didn't answer my prayer. When he didn't answer I decided I wanted no more of God and I turned away from him. I'm sorry. I'm so sorry.' she cried. 'I really want to follow Jesus and witness for him.'

"When we were through praying, she called the women to come back into the room and she told them all that had happened. They hugged and kissed her and then formed a circle. There was more repenting and praying until everyone went home rejoicing."

When Alice finished I sat silently for awhile thinking of all she had told me. "Those weren't failures. They were wonderful successes," I said.

"Some would call it failure because I didn't get the thing I went to pray for. Each time I had to pray for something different, and the answer was different."

"In each instance you would have prayed for the obvious if you hadn't listened for the right prayer. It seems evident that when you pray the right prayer, one that can be answered, the answer comes surprisingly fast."

Alice was looking at me with astonishment. "You are always analyzing everything." she said.

"And you, don't you ever analyze?" I asked.

"No, I just spent a lot of time in prayer and things work out. I don't plan it that way."

"You seem to hear God's voice so much clearer than the rest of us. Why is that?"

"Before the vision I didn't hear like I do now. It seems to be a gift, but then it seems that the gift is given to those who are eager to spend a lot of time in prayer."

"How much time do you spend in prayer?" I asked.

"I guess I am praying or listening most of the time. I recognize his voice. I know when he is speaking to me."

We sat in silence as I struggled to frame a question that had haunted me since we had returned to Gaza. Finally I put the question simply. "Gaza isn't the same. There seems to be more tension, more hostility toward Israel. Is there going to be war?"

Alice seemed startled at my question, "Yes," she said finally, "yes, there will be war—not the final war—but there will be much trouble for the churches." There were many more questions I wanted to ask her, but the time was up and she had to leave if she were going to get a ride home.

I closed the door after her and leaned against it thinking of what she had said. It was so obvious I really didn't need Alice to tell me that there would be war. Every time I rode down to the beach I passed the barbed wire enclosure where young men were being recruited for the Palestine Liberation Army. This was new. It hadn't been there when we left to go home.

Inside the wire enclosure men huddled in close little groups talking, while on the outside their mothers, wives, and children clung to the fence crying. It had been reported that they were served only lentil soup and were trained in the desert to survive on wild herbs and snakes.

I shuddered at the thought of war. I almost wished I hadn't asked Alice about it. War would change everything. Who would start it? Certainly not the little band of Palestinians behind the wire fence, nor could I imagine Israel starting a war. Alice could be wrong. I hoped and prayed she was wrong.

CHAPTER
13

By December 1966 the rumors of impending war had escalated. Tension mounted with each day and took its toll as the nursing students complained of nausea, others on the compound developed ulcer-like symptoms, and each day saw more patients coming into the clinic with both nausea and headaches. For the first time in years the word *war* was spoken seriously.

Christmas came and with it our children from Alexandria. For one month we tried to forget the news and devoted ourselves to making Christmas special. Gaza was totally Moslem except for the few Greek Orthodox citizens, and they celebrated at a different time and in a different way. Therefore, while our homes and the hospital would be gay with lights and decorations brought from home or made by hand, the rest of Gaza outside the hospital walls would be going about its business in the usual way.

As in other years our whole family went out to the Shawa orange grove to pick out our Christmas tree, then came back to have a party that included the student nurses. We sang carols, strung the lights brought from home, and decorated the tree with treasured ornaments and homemade cookies.

Alice came by to admire the tree and to relax for a few moments without having to think of the news or the tension that was building just outside the hospital walls. "Is there really going to be war?" I asked her, as I rearranged some of the lights on the tree.

"Some say war is inevitable," she said, "the only question is how or when."

"And what do you think?" I asked.

She hesitated, and when she answered there seemed to be a great sadness in her voice. "Everyone thinks a war would make things better, but it isn't true." There was more she wanted to say but instead she shrugged. What good would speculation do? The chain of events that would determine the future were already in place.

The excitement of having our children home and the joy of the Christmas celebration anesthetized us to the news. Instead, we plunged into the big dinner for all the hospital employees, with boxes of chocolates for each one brought from Beirut and given out by a Santa Claus so well disguised that even our children didn't recognize their own father beneath the white beard.

Choirs were formed and pageants staged with our children and the nurses, student nurses, and young people from town taking part. As in other years soldiers in the United Nations peace-keeping forces who made a habit of worshiping with us during the year came to celebrate and invited us to their celebrations. Men from Canada, Sweden, Norway, India, and Argentina added much to the Christmas spirit with their songs and shared traditions.

It almost seemed that the tables in our dining room were loaded higher with cakes and cookies than usual and more visitors from town came saying, *"Kul Sanna ou intu salem,"* the Christmas greeting. There was nostalgia in the air—some hint of the coming crisis that would make this Christmas memorable as the last to be enjoyed in just this way.

By the time Christmas and New Year were past and we were preparing to take the children back to the boarding school in Alexandria, we had decided to take a short furlough. "We will be leaving for the States as soon as school closes in May so you must work hard to bring your grades up," I cautioned the children before we left. Little did I know that within a few months our world would be falling apart and all plans for the future would be scrapped.

Just as the rains ended and the flowers in the formal gardens burst into a riot of color, things took a turn for the worse. The U.N.

secretary-general U Thant came on the radio to announce "an extremely tense and unstable" situation existing between the Arab and Israeli states that could erupt at any time.

In the weeks that followed the tension increased and our lives began to revolve around the regular reports of the news on the radio. Television was unheard of in the Gaza Strip or Middle East, so the outside world came to us only two times a day in brief, terse statements from the British Broadcasting System and the "Voice of America."

There would be the crackling sound as we turned on the set and then the jolly ditty that always introduced the news. "Arabs continue to work on their project to divert the waters of the Jordan River and Prime Minister Levi Eshkol of Israel talks of adopting drastic measures," the voice had the clipped, efficient British accent that lent authenticity to the news.

"Border clashes escalate. Israeli pilots down six Syrian jets." On and on it went, getting closer and closer to some sort of confrontation.

On May 15 I was up at 6:00 AM having my devotional in a little shelter of palm fronds we had fixed on our flat roof. It was a delightful place to hear the sounds of Gaza waking and watch the sun come up over the palm trees. On this morning the birds were singing, the air was fresh and cool, and it was impossible to imagine that anything as ominous as war could lie just across the border barely five miles away in Israel.

I turned to the reading for the day in *Daily Strength for Daily Needs* and was encouraged by the Bible verse, "My presence shall go with thee, and I will give thee rest" (Ex. 33:14).

Since we were leaving for our short furlough within the next few weeks, I appropriated the verse and its meaning for our ride to pick up the children from school and then for our trip back to our home in Washington, D.C. It had been three-and-a-half years since we had left the United States for the second time, and we were looking forward to catching up with our families and spending time with our children.

Just five days later everything had changed and it became evident that as superintendent of the hospital and surgeon, David would be needed and we would not be leaving Gaza for at least another year.

Egyptian President Nasser had ordered the UNEF soldiers to leave their peace-keeping posts at Sharm-el-Sheik at the tip of the Sinai Peninsula and all Israeli shipping stopped in the gulf. There was no doubt now that, short of a miracle, war was inevitable.

As the clouds of war gathered some of our friends stayed away and others avoided talking to us. "It's the anti-American feeling." they explained, "If there is war with Israel, we know what side America will take and you are Americans."

In all of this confusion Alice was unchanged. She still came and went much as always. She ignored what people might say and offered her help and friendship. "What are you going to do about your children in Egypt?" she asked me late one afternoon.

"Ann Nicholas and I had planned to drive to Alexandria to pick them up but now that's impossible. I hear the whole area is bristling with tanks and armored trucks."

"It would be dangerous to go alone like that," she said. "You'd better take the train."

"I hate to think of it. The only time I ever rode on the train it was a long, hot ride with hard seats and windows that wouldn't shut so the soot and sand got in our hair and even in our luggage."

"It's not easy, but it's the only way now."

"You're right, it won't be easy bringing all the children's belongings home on the train. Just think of the tennis racquets, books, souvenirs, posters, and who knows what else they will think they have to take."

It was finally decided that we would go to Alexandria on the train. We had our tickets and the permits needed to leave Gaza, our bags were packed, when suddenly the unexpected happened.

"Mrs. Dorr, there is bad news." Alice's voice sounded faint and far away and I could hear horns honking and voices scolding in the background. I wondered where Alice was calling from. "The train can't go to Cairo anymore. The tracks have been blown up."

Just as we were assimilating this news a message from the school arrived through the United Nations headquarters, "All Americans ordered to leave Egypt. School closed. Dorr and Nicholas children being sent to Beirut."

This news threw us into a frenzy of anxiety. We wondered if our children would remember how to get to the mission's school in Beirut. Could they manage getting in and out of airports in a foreign country without the help of an adult? And money—did they have enough to buy tickets? Could they use Egyptian money in Beirut? There was so many unknowns and we were so helpless.

A mission meeting was held and we discussed every angle of our situation. The wives and children of the U.N. staff had already been evacuated and we were told that the last U.N. plane would leave on Sunday, May 28, just one week away. The U.N. officials urged that all women and children in our organization be flown out at that time. Whatever the others might decide I knew that I would have to go, if for no other reason than to try to find our children in Beirut.

Everyone was jittery and some were sick with various nervous ailments. We all hoped to wake up and find this was a bad dream but instead the news got worse and worse. The American Sixth Fleet was moved into the Mediterranean and at the same time the Russians sent ten ships from the Black Sea.

Sunday morning May 21 started off as usual with the early call of the muezzin from a nearby mosque. Then came the sound of honking horns and blaring music interspersed with loud, political announcements from the coffee houses as Gaza gradually came to life.

There was a new tension in the air that even the deep tones of the Greek Orthodox Church bell or our own more insistent one couldn't disguise. People coming to the morning service in our chapel stood in tight little knots in the courtyard discussing the possibilities of war. They seemed reluctant to go in. They didn't want to be caught off guard in case there was some new development.

Alice wasn't there. She was be teaching school. She was the only person I knew that went about her business much as usual, and I knew she would be at the evening service.

When she got out of the taxi, just inside the big, green gate, she wasn't smiling. It was obvious she didn't want to talk. Instead, she went into the chapel and sat down off to one side alone. I could tell that she was disturbed.

I looked around at the familiar scene. Each face belonged to someone loved and special. The old-fashioned pump organ playing the familiar tunes gave an air of stability that belied the apprehension we all felt. Would we ever sit together like this again? If war came, as seemed probable, I wondered how our lives would be changed. Would we ever meet again just like this?

David was leading the singing and then the prayer. I couldn't concentrate on what he was praying because of the paralyzing fear of what lay in store for us. It had now been decided that David and Merrill Moore would be staying. That meant that I would be going to Beirut without him. We still had heard no word from the children who had left Egypt several days before. We were completely cut off from them. In the same way, once I left there would be no way of knowing what was happening at the hospital nor would David know where we were. My heart began to pound, and I found myself blotting the sweat that broke out on my forehead. I was frightened, genuinely frightened.

The final song was sung and we all went out into the soft gathering darkness. No one spoke as each was lost in his or her own thoughts. I hardly noticed when Alice fell into step with me. "Did you see what happened during the prayer?" she asked.

"No," I said, "I had my head bowed and was praying."

"Then you missed it."

"Missed what?" I said as I became aware of her smiling face.

"Jesus. He was there. He was there in our midst."

"Yes, I know. " 'Where two or three are gathered together. . . .' "

"No, no, not like that. I saw him and one of the nurses saw him too. He was here in person."

I stopped and looked at her quizzically. "What do you mean?"

"During the prayer while your husband was praying Jesus appeared beside him. We saw him as clearly as I see you now. He was stretching out his hands like in blessing over us, first to the left, then the middle, and finally to the right."

I could see that Alice was no longer worried. It was obvious that something had happened. "But what does it mean?" I asked. "Why did he come?"

"Don't you see? It's obvious. We're not to worry. These will be difficult days but he will protect us. Not one of us will be harmed." For once I didn't cross-examine her. I simply accepted what she had told me at face value. Jesus had been there when we needed him most. I hadn't seen him but Alice and Sameha had, and that was all that mattered.

Alice had to hurry to ride home in the van. She turned and was still smiling as she waved. It was obvious that she was no longer afraid.

Now big tanks rolled in, trenches were dug, and guns were issued to all civilians. Houses were boarded up, extra food bought and stored, water supplies checked, bomb shelters readied. Finally it was announced that there would be a trial blackout, and we were told to take shelter underground if possible.

Jimmy, John, and I carried candles, blankets, and drinking water to the basement below my small office across the courtyard from our house. The children were terribly frightened as we sat in the total darkness and heard the roar of tanks and the sputtering of machine-gun fire. "Where is Daddy?" they asked.

"He is in the hospital. Everyone has to be in place just as though the war had begun."

"Where are Philip and Paul and Debby?"

"I hope they are in Beirut. We will find out Sunday when we get there."

May 28, the fatal day, had arrived. In a daze I had packed and repacked our suitcases so they would meet the rigid U.N. requirement for weight. A kind of numbness had settled over me as I tried to think of everything that must be done before leaving. Only those who absolutely had to stay to keep the hospital running were to be left and that had narrowed down to the two doctors, David and Merrill Moore.

We struggled to keep our spirits up on the way to the small airfield, but even when we climbed on board and fastened the seat belts it seemed unreal. The usual seats had been replaced by more practical long, narrow benches that ran down each side of the plane. I held Jimmy on my lap and we looked out the window opposite us. There on the far side of the airstrip was Israel, so close we could see the buildings and fields of the kibbutz. We turned and looked out the window behind us to see the small picket fence and shed that made up our airport. David and Merrill with a few others from the hospital were waving.

"What's going to happen to Daddy?" Jimmy asked.

My eyes clouded with tears, and it was some moments before I could answer him, "He'll be all right," I heard myself saying. "God will take care of him."

Immediately the fear rose up, and I wondered that I had been able to say such a thing with the ring of assurance. It was Alice that saw Jesus, not me, and Alice that knew what his coming meant. However, again and again, as the war broke out and we moved from Beirut to Istanbul and then to Rome I thought of the vision Alice had that last Sunday night. Jesus had been there in our midst and that somehow made all the difference.

Despite the comfort I had received from Alice's prediction, it was well I didn't hear of the one near casualty until much later. On the second day of the war when mortars were being exchanged between the Palestinians on the beach and the Israelis at the border, David had a close call.

He had been giving out ration cards. On the first day of the war over two-hundred-and-fifty people had fled to the hospital seeking shelter. They also needed food, so a rationing system had been initiated by Youseph Khouri. Every family was given a card that had to be presented when they came for meals. It was these cards David was carrying when he was suddenly called to see a patient.

Impulsively, he set the cards down on the cement ledge that bordered the reservoir and hurried into the clinic. Almost immediately there was the sharp, whistling sound and then the ear-splitting blast of the explosion as a mortar fell directly on the spot where he had been standing just a moment before. It blew the cards in every direction and killed a donkey hitched to a cart just a few feet away.

Later as Alice was telling me the story of those days she said, "There were some close calls as the mortars fell on the compound from both the Egyptian guns at the beach and the Israeli guns on the border. Most of us were huddled in the basement below the hospital kitchen or in the new nurses' home. Windows were shattered and a gardener's leg broken but no one was killed. Jesus was with us and not one person that had been in the chapel that Sunday night had been hurt." They had been through pain, loss, pounding mortars, and the humiliation of defeat but they were alive.

Much more could be written of this time. It was a time of great upheaval and change. Some of the changes were so subtle that they were not recognized at first, others were all too obvious. When permission finally came for me to return to Gaza, I was shocked to realize that I would be flying into Tel Aviv and would drive from there to Gaza. The road that had always been blocked by a guardhouse and U.N. soldier was now open. We could drive to Gaza from Israel.

CHAPTER
14

Riding back into Gaza was a strange experience. Now instead of flying from Beirut or driving from Egypt we were actually driving from Tel Aviv in Israel. Both Lebanon and Egypt were closed to us. Before the war we had lived as though we were on an island five miles wide and twenty-five miles long. Now suddenly we were joined to a whole land mass with even Jerusalem within driving distance. It gave us a peculiar, disoriented feeling.

More than six weeks had passed since we had been evacuated, and as we neared Gaza we were shocked to see so many signs of the fighting still evident: burned-out tanks left at the side of the road, gutted buildings attesting to the strength of the mortars on both sides, and many shops with their garage-like doors pulled down and locked. The streets were full of Israeli soldiers standing at street corners and on buildings, their helmets and olive-green uniforms looking out of place in the town that had known mostly flowing robes, or the *tarbooshes* and *kaffieyehs* of its Arab residents.

Just as strange were the women who now crowded the sidewalks. Where Bedouins with coins dripping from their headbands, refugees in embroidered dresses with half-covered faces, or the town women with their black cloaks and gauzy black head coverings had once walked, we now saw only the sleeveless, miniskirted Israeli women who had come down on a bus to see what Gaza was like.

In place of camels, donkey carts, and Mercedes there were half-tracks, lorries, and a few tanks bristling with guns.

Some of the shops were open and their owners were inside, but they weren't smiling and no small cups of coffee were being offered to anyone. The vendors on the street who sold the rainbow-colored ice cream and the *falaffel* were nowhere to be seen. No music blared from the tightly closed coffeehouse. Apart from the tourists who crowded the streets it was a city of the dead.

As our car turned into the hospital compound people, nodded a greeting and stood in little clumps of interest, but no one smiled. One by one they came to tell us how glad they were that we had come back and how grateful they were that the American doctors had stayed to help them. Each had a story to tell. Each, in the six days of the war, had had their lives torn apart so they would never be the same.

The lazy, friendly little city of Gaza was gone forever, and its residents would remember the prewar days, even with its difficulties, nostalgically.

Alice came and it was from her I learned much of what had happened at the hospital during the war. "Do you remember," she asked, "how Jesus appeared that last Sunday night in the chapel?"

"Yes," I said, "of course I remember."

"It was to encourage us. We suffered many things but no one was killed. Your husband came closest. If he had been standing there just a moment longer."

We both were silent thinking of the near disaster. I had served Alice a cup of Turkish coffee. She took a sip and then set it down. It was just as she had asked, without sugar and bitter. "It doesn't taste very good without sugar," I suggested. "Don't you want me to make you another cup?"

"No," she said, "A Gazawee's coffee always gives a hint of his feelings and ours are bitter now with defeat."

"The whole time we were gone we had no news of Gaza or what was happening here," I said. "Even our embassy in Rome couldn't help us. The vision you had of Jesus was a great comfort."

Alice, like others in Gaza, seemed stunned not only at the defeat but at all the changes it had made in their lives. "Everything is different," she said. "The Israelis have changed everything."

I had to admit that unbelievable changes had taken place. "For instance," I said, "we don't know where the children will go to school. It seems they will be going to the American International School in Tel Aviv, but it is too far to drive every day and right now there is no boarding section."

Alice was immediately alert. "Your children will be going up to Israel to school?"

"We don't know what to do. They can't go to Egypt or Lebanon now."

She seemed uneasy, as though there was something she felt she must say. "Can't you teach them like you did before?"

"They are too old. We have to find some way of getting them to a proper school, and there are only a few weeks left before school opens, and we still don't know what we are going to do."

Alice looked worried. "We know the problem," I assured her. "If they go up to Tel Aviv, even if it is an American school, it will look as though we are cooperating, won't it?" Alice didn't answer, but I knew that's what she was concerned about.

"We're asking advice from some of our friends," I said. "There has to be some way."

The school situation was finally solved. Some of our close Arab friends assured us they understood our problem and Ethne Stainer, one of the nurses from Australia, volunteered to go as a dorm parent. At the same time the mission in Israel rented a house near the school which would serve as a dormitory. It was finally decided that the four older children would go to school in Israel and Jimmy would be taught at home.

It was good that they were gone at this time. Gaza was in constant turmoil. Each day there was some disaster. An Israeli jeep would be blown up, old land mines accidently stepped on, hand grenades found by children playing, and many other things that brought people unexpectedly to the hospital.

Some of the trouble was brought on by an immediate clash of cultures. East and West had met on the streets of Gaza in the form of tourists wearing miniskirts eight inches above the knee and at the beach by brown, bikini-clad Israeli girls. The immediate response was shock. Then young men took over with sly pinches that not only made the girls squeal but brought out reporters and soldiers.

It was not long until there were horror stories making the rounds of Israeli soldiers beating up Gaza's young men. Shopkeepers pulled down their shutters and closed their shops in protest, declaring the strip closed to outsiders.

When the tension cleared and the shops reopened, Israeli women were warned to dress modestly, no minis and no swimming on Gaza beaches.

It was evident that though the mortars had stopped falling and tanks no longer rumbled through the streets, there was to be little peace in Gaza. There were constant provocations from the inhabitants and retaliation from the army. Some of the provocations took the form of blowing up Israeli vehicles, setting land mines, or holding demonstrations on Omar Mikhtar Street.

Retaliation took many forms, but one of the favorite in the camps was to declare a curfew. At such times no one was allowed outside their house for as long as the curfew lasted. It was in just such a situation that once again disaster struck, and Alice found herself drawn into the center.

It was late in the afternoon when suddenly I was aware of the frantic honking of horns mingled with hysterical weeping and wailing. Several Israeli land rovers filled with soldiers careened in through the big green gate. They were quickly followed by a large truck filled with people who seemed to be kneeling around a covered form. Behind the truck came a crowd of screaming women and angry men, shaking their fists and shouting in a threatening way.

"What is it?" I asked one of the student nurses. "What has happened?"

She shifted the books she was carrying to her other arm and leaned over to cautiously whisper. "Hadn't you heard? A young, ten-year-old girl was shot in the head by an Israeli soldier. They say if she dies all of Gaza will riot."

"How did it happen? Where was she?"

"They say she was visiting in the refugee camp with friends when a curfew was announced. She couldn't go home. The curfew lasted several days, and the family she was staying with grew short of water. They reasoned that the Israelis wouldn't shoot a little girl, so they put the water jar on her head and sent her out to get water."

"She was shot?"

"Yes, the bullet hit her in the forehead and then tore through her skull." Tears came to her eyes and she put the back of her hand to her mouth to keep from crying. "She isn't expected to live."

"Do you think the Israeli soldier just intended to shoot the jar?"

"Who knows?"

"Will she die?"

"There's really no hope. If she should live she will never be the same. A bullet tearing up her brain like that, you can just imagine. It's awful but just about as bad will be the anger of people if she dies."

It was long after sunset when David came from the hospital. He still had his scrub suit on and was looking very tired. His stethoscope dangled from his pocket and slid to the floor as he sank into one of the dining room chairs. I had reheated the soup, but he wasn't hungry. "Did you see the little girl that got shot in the head?" I asked.

"Yes, in the midst of a dozen other crises."

"Did you operate on her?"

"It doesn't call for an operation. I debrided the wound and . . ."

"One of the nurses said the bullet went right through her head. Is that true?"

"It didn't go right through but along the top of her head tearing up the skull as it went. All along the groove the brain was oozing out. It wasn't a pretty sight."

"What will happen to her? Does she have a chance?"

He shook his head. "She will probably develop meningitis and die." We didn't discuss it anymore but I couldn't forget the little girl. Even when I went to bed that night I was haunted by thoughts of her. It didn't sound as though she would live until morning, and I wondered what would happen then. All those angry people were just waiting for something like this. The next day everyone was talking about the little girl. She was just barely alive, and all of us expected to hear the bad news at any moment that she had died.

Late afternoon came and Alice appeared at the door of my little workroom across the small courtyard from our house. "Have you heard about the little girl from the refugee camp who was shot in the head?" I asked.

"Of course," Alice said, and I noticed she was smiling.

"Have you been to the hospital?" I asked, as I held open the door and invited her to come in.

"Yes." Alice said. There was a suppressed excitement that made me realize Alice wanted to tell me something, but she was afraid of my reaction.

I had been working on an article, and as we talked I gathered up the papers and put them in a folder. "Of course, you have seen the little girl. You know there is no chance for her to live?" A strong suspicion was growing within me that Alice might have gone and prayed for the little girl, may have even thought she could be healed. I wanted to warn her that this was impossible.

"Yes, I saw her and talked with her mother." There was still that undefined element of excitement that crept into her voice as she talked about it.

"Alice!" I said, "you didn't encourage the mother I hope." My voice was stern and the smile on Alice's face disappeared.

"The mother was crying."

"And the little girl?"

"She was unconscious."

"But you're smiling. What happened? What did you do?"

Alice hesitated, but she didn't look intimidated or embarrassed by the tone of my voice.

"I asked the mother if she wanted me to pray for her little girl. I told her I only prayed in Jesus' name."

"And . . .?" The concern must have been evident on my face because Alice hesitated and for a moment I thought she wasn't going to tell me any more.

"I prayed and God showed me that if the mother had faith the little girl would be healed." Alice spoke quickly as though wanting to get it all out before I stopped her with my reaction.

"And you told her that?"

"Of course."

"Does anyone else know about this?"

"Yes, I guess all the women on the ward know because the mother was so happy she wanted to tell everyone."

"Oh, Alice!" I groaned. "Did you have to tell her?"

Again I could see that Alice was disappointed in me. "She has faith and the little girl will be healed," Alice insisted. "You will see."

That was all we said about the little girl. Alice told me a few incidents that had happened at school and then it was time to go. She insisted I not get up, that she could let herself out. As I rolled a new sheet of paper in the typewriter I tried not to think about the little girl or Alice, but it was impossible. I was worried. Certainly, this time Alice had acted impulsively. Had she really heard the voice of the Lord? If not it could be disastrous in many ways.

Later when David came home from the hospital I asked about the girl. "Is she better? Have you noticed any improvement?"

"No," he said. "In fact, she's worse. The wound has become infected. It's really a terrible-looking sight with pus pouring out. She isn't expected to live through the night."

I felt the icy fingers of fear grip my heart. This was going to be one time Alice was wrong. Why did it have to be in a situation that all Gaza was watching? Certainly there were those outside the women's ward who by this time knew what Alice had said. They would also be watching to see what happened. I determined to contact Alice as soon as possible and warn her not to encourage the mother further.

The next day about the same time Alice stopped by to report

that she had once again gone to visit the mother. "She was standing by the bed holding her little girl's hand," Alice said.

"I hope you didn't encourage her," I said. "The wound is infected. It's hopeless."

Alice grew silent and pensive. "I'm not going on how the child
looks. I'm depending on what the Lord showed me when I prayed,
and he showed me that if the mother had faith her little girl would
be healed."

"Even though her daughter hasn't regained consciousness, the
mother still believes?" I asked.

"Yes, her faith is strong. She believes her daughter will be
healed."

"But Alice," I countered, my voice almost sounding desperate,
"If her daughter isn't healed, she will lose her faith completely."

"That is not my concern. I can only tell her what I saw when I
prayed."

"There are quite a few other people who also know you have
said the little girl will be healed. Just think what a blow to their
faith it will be if the little girl dies."

Alice looked sad. "Why can't you believe?" she asked.

"I guess," I said hesitantly, "it's because it is so hopeless. Her
skull has been ripped open by the bullet and now it is infected."

CHAPTER
15

A week went by and still the little girl remained in a coma, but now I began to hear reports from people who had heard that Alice had prayed for her. "How can she tell that mother her daughter will be healed when it is obvious the child can't live?" they questioned.

"Alice isn't just claiming a Bible verse like some people do, nor is she going on wishful thinking," I said, trying to defend her.

"Whatever she's doing, it's wrong," one of the nurses said. "She has the mother's hopes all built up and it's evident that even if the little girl should live she will have such brain damage she will never be normal."

The nurse left and I was again in a turmoil. What good would it do for the little girl to live if she were going to be brain damaged? I determined that I would talk to Alice again. Certainly she hadn't thought of this. She had explained to me that she came every day to be sure the mother's faith was not undermined. When she came I must make her see that this was not the usual situation.

I did have some concern as I thought of the people who had promised to riot if the child died. That would be unfortunate for all of us. It would deepen the anger and resentment but it could not be helped. It was not as though everything medically possible had not been done for her.

The next day when Alice came from the hospital, I was waiting for her. I had been talking to some of the student nurses and they had also told me of their concern. "You must talk to Alice," they said. "She doesn't understand. She doesn't know anything about medicine or she would see that this is hopeless."

Alice was again smiling, and I could see that it was not going to be easy to discourage her. "Alice," I began, but she held up her hand in a "wait-a-minute" gesture.

"You're worried about the little girl. I know she's just the same but the mother, you should see her; she has such faith."

"Oh Alice," I said, almost in despair. "You don't understand. This is different. The wound is infected now."

"Yes. I know. They told me that at the hospital. I'm not depending on how the little girl looks. I only know the Lord told me that if the mother has faith in Jesus' ability to heal her daughter her daughter will be cured."

"Alice, I understand but, . . ."

"Why do you have to always add 'but'?"

"Because I am seeing the whole situation."

Alice grew thoughtful as though she was desperately trying to see things through my eyes. "You are like the disciples in the storm on the Sea of Galilee. They looked at the storm and were frightened because they forgot that Jesus was in the boat."

"Don't misunderstand me, Alice. I do believe that there is nothing impossible with God. I've even had many prayers answered, but this is somehow different."

"How?"

"The little girl is obviously dying, and now the nurses tell me that even if she should live her brain is so damaged she will never be right mentally. Doesn't that worry you?"

"No. That is not my business. I prayed, and the Lord showed me that if the mother had faith her daughter would be healed. I don't heal. I am only the messenger, but I don't believe Jesus does things halfway. You will see. She will be all right."

A week later there was still no change and I went to the hospital to see the little girl and her mother for myself. There was a screen around the bed at one end of the ward and a woman, obviously the mother, sat in a chair with her head cradled in her arms. I knew she must be weak with exhaustion. The child carefully covered by a sheet with only her bandaged head showing. There was no movement. The child lay in a deep coma as though she were dead.

"*Ahlan, Ahlan wa sahlan!*" I was startled by a greeting that seemed to come from the other side of the screen. I quickly moved around to where I could see a young woman lying in bed swathed in bandages. "There's no change yet," she said nodding toward the screen.

"You must be the young woman who was so badly burned." I remembered hearing about her when I saw the bandages. I even knew that her name was Assiyah.

"Yes, they didn't think I would live. I really didn't want to live." She had been the second wife of an older man. The first wife couldn't have any children, so he had married Assiyah. Almost immediately she became pregnant and from that moment on she had nothing but trouble with the older wife. When the baby was born the older woman in a fit of jealousy killed the baby by smothering it. Assiyah was wild with grief. She tried to end her life by throwing herself in the fire.

"Are you feeling better?" I didn't know quite what else to say.

"Yes, much better. I will go home at the end of this month."

There was a movement on the other side of the screen and a small, very pleasant-faced woman stood looking at me. "I'm Fareeda's mother," she said.

I hadn't known before that the little girl with the bullet wound's name was Fareeda. "How is she?" I asked.

"The doctors and nurses say she is very bad. They don't have any hope but there is a woman who came. . . ."

"Yes, I know," I said. "Her name is Alice."

The woman's face broke into smiles, and I could see she was actually quite young. It was just the wrinkles in her face that made her look older. "Yes, she is a wonderful woman. She comes every day." She motioned for me to come around the screen to where I could see her daughter.

I stood beside the bed and looked down at the chalk-white face;

the bandages covered her whole head and forehead, her eyes were closed and her mouth relaxed. Her mother picked up her hand, and I noticed that it rested limp and lifeless in her own warm, brown one. "Are you here all the time?" I asked.

"Yes. I want to be here when she wakes up so she won't be frightened."

It was evident the woman was taking for granted that her daughter would wake up. Tears came to my eyes, and I found that I couldn't say anything. I turned away and saw Sameha, one of the student nurses, had come to check her temperature. "Is she any better?" I asked. She didn't answer but shook her head and mouthed the word, *no.*

I turned quickly, said good-bye to the mother, and hurried out of the ward.

Sameha followed me out onto the balcony, "I hope Alice is right, but it really looks bad."

"Yes, it is amazing the mother has such faith."

Sameha's face fell. "I don't have faith like that. I wish I did."

I made an effort to change the subject. "You graduate this year don't you? We'll really miss you. I don't know anyone more loved by the patients."

"I hope I graduate."

"What do you mean hope? Of course you'll graduate."

To my surprise Sameha began to cry. "I don't know. You know I had to repeat last year. This is my last chance."

"Everybody feels that way. If you just study hard everything will be all right."

"No, no, you don't understand. I have studied. I knew it last year, but I was so frightened when I came to take the test that my mind just went blank. Now I am worse. I can't take tests."

"Is it the English that is so hard for you?" I knew it must be very difficult for the nursing students to have all their lessons and tests in English.

"The English is difficult, but it isn't that. I never have been able to take tests, and now it's worse. I can know everything perfectly the day before, but when I go to take a test I can't remember even my name."

I was really concerned now because I knew that our new nursing instructor had set very high standards and wouldn't be likely to make exceptions. "You don't have much time to prepare."

"I know," she said. "I asked Alice to pray for me."

"What did she say?"

"She said that if I had faith in Jesus then I would pass. The trouble is I don't have faith. I am a Christian, have been all my life, but I don't really have faith like that little woman in there."

"I suppose Alice is meeting with you every day for prayer."

"Yes, when she is with me I have the faith that it is possible, but within a few hours it is gone and I am frightened again."

I gave her a hug and another tissue to wipe her tears. "I'll be praying for you too, Sameha." I said. "Somehow it's not so hard for me to believe you will be able to do well on the test as it is to believe Fareeda can be healed."

Alice didn't come by for several weeks, and though I saw her at Sunday evening church services and at Wednesday night prayer meeting we both avoided the subject of Fareeda. From David and the nurses I heard that Fareeda had gotten worse and then to their surprise she rallied. "There's still no hope for her recovery but she's passed some kind of a crisis. She'll probably live, but not regain consciousness."

I was again in the little back room I used as a study when I heard a loud, insistant knocking on the patio gate. I hurried out and undid the complicated latch, opened the door, and saw Alice smiling and so happy I knew she had some very good news.

"I don't have time to stop and talk," she said. "But guess what has happened? Fareeda opened her eyes today. She recognized her mother and said, 'Umi' (mother). Isn't that wonderful?"

"Yes, it is wonderful. No one expected her to ever talk again and certainly not recognize anyone."

"Of course it's not the whole healing, but it is the beginning."

A week later the parents of Fareeda took her home and I lost track of her. She hadn't died but neither had she been what I would call healed. I hated to ask Alice any more questions. I felt it would be too embarrassing.

Two months passed, and one Friday near the end of November Alice again appeared at the door smiling. "Can you come, Mrs. Dorr?"

"Come! Where?"

"I want to take you out to see Fareeda. It isn't far. They live in the midst of an orange grove her father has. I have a taxi waiting."

There were many things I had planned to do but I quickly decided this was more important. "Is she any better?" I asked as I picked up the phone to call Marian Jenner, the nurse from Australia.

"You will see." Alice was evasive, but I could tell by her smile and the twinkle in her eyes that she had a surprise.

When I told Marian what I was going to do, she quickly agreed to go along. She had been the nurse in charge of the ward when Fareeda first came in, and I felt she would also be interested in her progress.

The taxi took us to the edge of town, then along a dirt road lined with cactus until at last we came to a small orange grove. The oranges were bright bits of captured sunshine against the green leaves, and it made a pretty sight. "Here, is where we stop." Alice motioned for the driver to park opposite an enclosure of cactus. Rising above the cactus was a mud-walled house with a small courtyard and several rooms that appeared to be empty. In the enclosure were many cows.

"*Ahlan, Ahlan.*" Now I saw that there was a crudely formed gate that opened in the midst of the cactus. Standing to greet us in the opening was the woman I had seen in the hospital with a young girl by her side. Alice rushed forward and embraced the mother and the girl.

"This is Fareeda," she said, drawing back and looking with pride at the little girl.

I was completely taken aback. The girl was smiling shyly and she put out her hand. As I took it I noticed the other arm hung limp by her side. It was the only evidence of the ordeal she had just been through other than the close-cropped curls that covered her head. Her whole head had been shaved to treat the wound, and the hair was just beginning to grow again.

The mother excused herself while Fareeda took us to see the orange grove. As she pointed out the various trees and their burden of fruit, her shyness left and she became quite talkative. Alice encouraged her by asking questions, and as she answered Alice would nod to us with a pleased look on her face as if to say, "See, didn't I tell you?"

As we were coming back to the little house we met a woman swinging along with a basket on her head. Only when we got closer did we see that she had a baby in the basket. She stopped and took Fareeda by the arm. "Where are your guests from?" she asked.

"They are from the Baptist Hospital," Fareeda told her.

Upon hearing this the woman broke into a smile, "I was a patient in that hospital last year," she said. "Bring them to visit me. I would be so honored to have them."

Fareeda spoke very quickly, "There isn't time. My mother is preparing something for them."

The woman didn't say anything but followed us back, and lifting the basket from her head, she cradled the baby in her arms. When it cried she wiped its nose with the end of her mantle and brought out one breast to silence him with the warm milk.

We found that Fareeda's mother had taken a new blanket that had been bought for the occasion and had spread it under the trees. She had borrowed folding chairs and a table which she had placed on the blanket in the shade. She motioned for us to remove our shoes and sit in this place of honor on the blanket. There were three chairs, one for each of us. Fareeda stood beside Alice, all the time answering questions Alice put to her. "Do you remember how I taught you to thank God for your food?" Alice said, as we bowed our heads for the blessing before eating the pigeons and rice the mother had prepared.

"Yes, I remember," Fareeda said as she bowed her head and repeated the prayer along with Alice.

When the platter of food was removed, Alice talked for a few moments about school. "I heard you could not get into school. They didn't believe you could do the work?" Alice asked.

"Yes, I am having trouble. They can't believe I am all right."

"I will talk to the headmistress tomorrow," Alice said. "They can give you a test and that will remove their doubt."

Fareeda smiled. She had missed school and was eager to get back.

"Fareeda," Marian said. "When you were unconscious did you ever hear what was being said around you."

For a moment she seemed to stop and think and then she said, "Sometimes."

"What did you hear?" Marian asked again.

"I heard Sitt Alice tell my mother she would pray in Jesus' name and I would be healed."

"Did you know who Jesus was?"

"No."

"Did you think about being healed."

"No, I just heard them talking and sometimes praying."

The father joined them to say "good-bye." He looked quite old with wrinkles and a prickly beard. One eye was swollen shut, and I noticed his sandals were tied together with string and his *galabia* was patched. "I want to pay you. You have given me back my daughter," the old man said looking at Alice with obvious appreciation.

"Who did I tell you healed her?" Alice said, drawing back and looking stern.

"Jesus, you said Jesus, but let us pay you for what you did."

Alice shook her head. "If I have any gift at all it is from God, and the moment I start to charge people the gift will be taken away."

We left them standing outside the cactus hedge, and just before I got into the car I looked back at the little group. The woman had put her baby back into the basket on top of her head and was

standing off to one side, the mother and father stood beside Fareeda and Fareeda was waving.

As we moved off in the car I asked Alice, "There is only one
more question."

Alice stiffened. She always thought I asked too many questions.
"You still have questions after you have seen her?" she said.

"Only one. When Fareeda has been so marvelously healed in so
many ways why is one arm still paralyzed?"

"Don't you know?"

"No, I have no idea."

"It is for a witness. In the future when people ask why her arm
is paralyzed, I have told her that she must tell them that she was
the little girl shot in the head after the 1967 war and was not
expected to live, but Jesus healed her."

No one said anything after that, and the taxi bounced and
bumped along on the rough track out of the orange grove and
turned on the smooth road back toward town.

I was astounded at what I had seen and heard. "Marian, you are
a nurse and have seen many strange things. Have you ever seen
anything quite like this?"

"No," Marian said. "It was as hopeless a case as I have seen. I
could hardly believe my eyes today. She hasn't even suffered any
brain damage."

Alice was sitting near the window saying nothing, but out of the
corner of my eye I could see that she was pleased.

CHAPTER
16

It was hard adjusting to the new Gaza. There were many surprises and one was tourists. We had never been able to have visitors because of the difficulty of getting in and out of Gaza. However, since the war, it had become the daring thing for tourists to do. They had heard of the biblical Samson's city, and now they wanted to see it. "If the tourists keep coming we will have to build some rest rooms for them," Ed Nicholas said. He was usually in the office near the gate, and he had been caught more often than the rest of us trying to solve the problems of tourists.

Curfews posed another problem. They could be called at any time, stranding people in unusual places and making it difficult to plan anything.

Explosions shattered the peace and never failed to catch us off guard. One Sunday after church David had decided to take a picture of the congregation. Everyone was in place and waiting for the flash to go off when suddenly there was a tremendous explosion that made the windows rattle and the floor shake. Some people started to dive for cover when they were reminded, "The Israelis are blowing up that man's house where they found all the ammunition."

Many Palestinian men from the camps were going to Jordan. They were afraid of being picked up for crimes they didn't commit. "It's hard to prove your innocence," one of the male nurses said after many from his camp had been rounded up and questioned.

It was at this time that some of us were invited to go to one of the camps to visit Assiyah, the patient that had been in the bed next to Fareeda. She was now divorced from the older man and living at home.

She was a natural entertainer and had a whole chain of events planned for us. "First you must all put on the fellahin dress and mantle," she said. She had gathered some lovely ones from her friends and we exclaimed over the yards of bright embroidery. When we were all finally dressed she brought us out into the small courtyard where she encouraged us to take pictures of our transformation.

For refreshments we were to have bread freshly baked on the rounded surface of an outdoor oven. When we were finally seated on carpets that had been spread out on the ground she handed each of us a *kazo* (soft drink).

While we were waiting for the bread, her brother showed us a scrapbook he had put together. He had gotten pictures from magazines and pasted them on the various pages, then had written out the conversations he imagined taking place. "I know all about Jesus," he volunteered. "I was in the hospital a long time ago when the British doctor, Dr. McClure, was here. He told me about Jesus."

Assiyah motioned to Marian. "Do you remember, Miss Jenner, the first day I came in and you talked to me?"

"Yes, but you were in such pain I didn't think you heard me."

"I heard. You said something about Jesus and then you told me that perhaps Alice would tell me more."

"I remember something like that." Marian said.

"Well, right after that they brought Fareeda in and I watched everything. I saw the doctors come in and discuss the problems. I could tell they didn't think she would live. Every day it was the same, and every day there was Alice telling the mother if she had faith her daughter would be healed. As you can imagine, I became very interested. I couldn't imagine what was going to happen. Finally I said to myself, *When I came in here I was almost dead, and I wanted to die because my baby was dead. I had no faith. I didn't even believe there was a God. But I determined that if Alice was right and Jesus had power to heal that little girl, then I wanted to know more about Him."*

She brought out a small Bible. "I have read this and I want to ask some more questions," she said. "Will you answer them for me?"

The rest of the afternoon was spent answering Assiyah's very astute questions. Finally when it was time for us to go she said, "I feel something new in my heart and I want it to grow. Can I come to the hospital to ask questions?"

"Of course, any of us would be glad to answer your questions."

It was getting dark, so reluctantly we took off the lovely, embroidered dresses and put on our own, then with many expressions of thanks we got into the car and headed for home.

"Alice," I said, as we got out of the car, "I have heard that you have told Sameha she will pass if she has faith and studies. Is that true?"

Alice looked surprised. "I didn't think you knew about that," she said. "Yes, when I prayed the answer came that if she studied and didn't lose her faith she could pass."

I had intended to say more, but then I remembered that this was just December and it would be spring before Sameha would face the tests she so dreaded. There would be plenty of time to talk about it later.

As the year progressed we found that not only had the war changed the city of Gaza, it had also curtailed most of the celebrations we had enjoyed at the hospital. Every year we had celebrated Halloween with a big costume party. It was something we worked on for weeks. All the doctors, nurses, student nurses, and friends in town were invited, but everyone had to wear some sort of costume. Not only did we think up costumes for ourselves and the children but often we had to come up with costumes for our guests. This year, after the war, for the first time we didn't have the costume party. "Gaza is in mourning," people explained to us. "We are wearing black and drinking bitter coffee; we aren't in any mood to celebrate."

Thanksgiving and Christmas were the same. "It wouldn't look right to have a tree with bright, happy lights and gay decorations," our friends told us. "No one will be visiting this year either," they added. "We just can't be happy in the midst of such defeat and misery."

We understood, and so we had none of the usual festivities. Our own tree was a very small one put up for the children in our bedroom. We had now been away from the United States almost four years, and our little stock of presents had gotten very low. Once again I closed the typewriter in the little study and pulled out the sewing machine. Almost everything anyone received would be homemade.

With Christmas came the first of the rains and the bitter cold. With no furnaces or fireplaces, we had only kerosene heaters to keep us warm. We pulled out sweaters and huddled around the vile-smelling kerosene heaters while David provided the only entertainment, with his popped corn and the reading of *The Little House on the Prairie.*

When Christmas was over and the children were ready to go back to school, they all thought it had been one of the nicest Christmases. "We didn't go home last summer for the short furlough as we had expected," David reminded them, "so we will be leaving for a year at home when school is out."

If December was cold, January and February were impossible. The only time I was really warm was when I was in bed with a hot water bottle. In spite of the cold David was restless and for the first time in his life began to wake up early before daylight. When he couldn't get back to sleep he would type letters.

We had many concerns, but most important was the problem that seemed to be rushing toward us at an unbelievable speed— where we were going to spend our furlough. We were already in some sort of a countdown, thinking of things we needed to take and things we needed to store, and yet we had no idea where we were going.

In the midst of this situation, Alice came to me after church and said, "Have you and Dr. Dorr been awake at night lately?" I was so surprised I didn't know what to say. Actually, it wasn't unusual for me to wake up, but it was for David, so I simply said, "I wake up a lot at night and can't get back to sleep."

"Well," said Alice, "the next time you and Dr. Dorr wake up you need to get out of bed and kneel down and pray. The Lord has shown me that he wants to talk to you."

"Alice!" I said with alarm. "It's too cold to get out of bed to pray. Can't we just pray in bed?"

"No!" she said very emphatically. "You are talking with the King of Glory and you must kneel down."

I thought about the whole thing a great deal. First, it was rather awesome that the Lord had shown Alice that he had something to say to us. In such a situation, like Adam and Eve, one begins to sort though all one's mistakes and bad attitudes to see if there is anything of that nature involved. Most of the day was gone before I realized that it could be something good he was wanting to tell us.

Next I wondered why at night when it was cold, we had to get out of bed. Why couldn't we just pray when David came home? I got no answer to that, but the reminder that Samuel was spoken to at night.

The whole thing was very strange. In fact, I kept coming back to the strangest part, how had Alice known that we were awake? How had she known that David was awake?

When David came home that night for dinner, I waited until he had eaten and then told him what Alice had said. "How did she know we were awake?" he asked right away. "Did you tell her?"

"No, no," I said. "That is what is so strange. She just knew."

"Why do we have to get out of bed to pray?"

"I asked Alice that, and she seemed to think it was disrespectful to lie in bed and pray. At least in this situation we must get out of bed and kneel down."

"Are we supposed to set the alarm clock?

"No, of course not. We do this only if we both happen to wake up again."

"What are we supposed to pray about?"

"I don't know. She simply says that the Lord has something to say to us."

David didn't answer. He seemed to accept it as a perfectly normal thing until bedtime when he asked again, "Are we supposed to do this crazy thing?"

"Only if we wake up."

With that we went soundly to sleep thinking that surely we would not both wake up. One o'clock came and I was awake thinking about the cold. Only my nose stuck out of the blankets and my feet were firmly clinging to the hot water bottle. I lay still, not wanting to wake David up. Only if we both woke up did we have to get out of bed. Now the idea of getting up in the cold far outweighed the curiosity of finding out what would happen if we did get up.

David yawned, then jabbed his pillow, and almost immediately was quiet, thinking. "Are you awake?" he asked finally.

"I'm awake," I said, almost in despair.

"And you think we really need to get out of bed and kneel down and pray."

"I think we'd better, though I can hardly stand to think of it."

"What are we praying about?"

"Anything that concerns us, but most of all we are supposed to listen."

"I can't listen very long in this cold." He said pushing back the blankets and easing himself out of the bed into his slippers and robe.

I put one foot out and pulled it back. The whole thing seemed so ridiculous when one got right down to doing it. In one brief moment all the characters of the Bible who were told to do something ridiculous passed through my mind. What if God really was there and wanted to talk to us? I certainly didn't want to take a chance on missing something like that.

In minutes I was out of bed, shivering as I pulled on my robe and wrapped a blanket around me before I knelt down. We thought of various concerns, the children at school, the problems in the hospital, and finally our furlough. Where were we to go?

"It's the furlough. I feel it is the furlough we are supposed to pray about. Maybe we're supposed to go some place where you can study to take the oral part of your boards."

"No. I told you I'm not going to put myself and the family under that much pressure."

"It's such a shame. You've passed the written and have only that oral left."

"You don't understand. Taking the oral after being out here and away from the academic world involves so much catching up to do it is impossible. That is out."

He said it with such feeling I knew it was decided in his mind and, yet, I couldn't help feeling it would be a great loss if he didn't finish. "Let's just pray about where we should go and only if the subject of taking the orals comes up will you consider it."

"There is no way the subject will just come up. To do this it would take someone finding a house we could afford, a car, and a program that would bring me up to date. To have all three just drop out of the blue is impossible. It just won't happen."

"Well, would you be willing to tell the Lord that if all these pieces did fall together you would accept it as His will that you study to pass your oral exam?"

He laughed, "There is no use talking about 'if'. It is totally impossible."

"Then, if it is impossible aren't you willing to say that if it should happen you would accept it as a sign."

"No, there is no way I'm going to take those boards."

"How can we ask God to show us his will if you have reservations about what you will do and won't do?"

He was silent, thinking it through. He knew it was limiting God to ask for his guidance and then put limitations on what would be acceptable. "All right," he said finally. "If we are offered a house we can afford, a salary supplement we can live on, and a car, and it all fits together in a program designed to prepare me for the orals I will do it. Don't be disappointed though. There is no chance of such a thing happening."

We got back into bed thinking that nothing much had happened. Only later could we look back and see what a turning point it had been.

Within the week David received a letter from his brother Bartlett in Richmond, Virginia, suggesting that both he and Dad Dorr thought David ought to study for his oral exam. They knew he would need some sort of study program, and Bartlett knew someone who would be willing to set up a program for him. At the same time some friends had a house they needed to rent furnished for the year, and Dad Dorr would make up the difference in the salary needed.

David was stunned. He hadn't believed it was possible and yet here, just a week after we had prayed, was the whole package put together. Without the commitment made that night he still would have turned it down but, as it was, he wrote and told Bartlett we would accept the plan and would be in Richmond that summer as soon as school was out.

Marian Jenner had worked with Sameha in the fall, but after she left to go to Kuwait, Sameha was on her own and depressed most of the time. Alice would pray with her and Sameha would begin to feel there was some hope, but before the week was out she was back in the pit of despair. "I took a short, little test today," she told Alice, "and I was terrified."

"What grade did you get on the test?"

"I barely made sixty." she said.

"And sixty is what you need to make in the small tests to pass."

"I have to make at least sixty on each of the small tests and eighty on the final. I can't do it." Sameha was again in tears.

Over and over, Alice would have to bolster up her faith. One time she came and found Sameha ready to pack and go home. "Someone has stolen your faith," Alice said. "I was praying for you at home, and I found that someone has stolen your faith."

"They have only tried to make me face reality. They don't want me to be upset if I don't pass."

Alice sank down in the chair beside Sameha's desk. "You can pass if you have faith. You must not let anyone steal your faith."

"But what if I fail?"

"If you fear the tests and think failure, you will fail. Only if you have faith will you pass."

As the time of testing drew near Alice came one day to the nurses' home and asked for Sameha. "We have to go to the dressmaker," she said. "You will need a dress for graduation."

Sameha looked smitten. "But what if . . .?"

"No what ifs," Alice said. "Faith prepares for the answer, and you will need the dress."

As they went down the hall they met some of the girls coming from the class. They wanted to know where Alice and Sameha were going. "I'm going to town," Sameha said, dodging the issue.

"To the dressmaker," Alice said.

"To the dressmaker?" the girls were immediately interested.

"Yes, she is going to pick out the cloth and be measured for her graduation dress." Sameha cringed and the girls grew silent, speculating on the turn of events. They all knew the problem Sameha had with tests and they knew the nursing director was not going to be easy on her.

"Alice!" Sameha said when they were well past the girls. "Did you have to say it was going to be my graduation dress?"

"Of course. It is going to be your graduation dress."

Sameha studied until her eyes were red, and the more she studied the more frightened she became. "Come pray with me Alice," she said, "It's just a few days until the tests and I am so afraid."

Alice went with her, saying she could only stay five minutes but an hour went by before she felt Sameha was all right again. "The Lord has shown me he wants you for a witness. He is going to bless you and you will pass." Alice spoke with such assurance that for the first time Sameha was almost confident. "Come now," Alice said. "We are going to buy the candy you will give out in celebration of your passing. Only instead of giving it out after the tests like everyone else you will give it out before."

"I can't, what if . . .?"

"No more what ifs," Alice insisted.

The day before the tests Sameha came rushing over to show me a letter she had gotten from Marian Jenner in Australia. The letter told how Marian had been showing slides in a church in Australia and there had been a picture of Sameha as one of the student nurses. Marian told of Sameha's struggle, and after the meeting a man came forward, "I know that God is going to use her. Don't worry. She will pass." Then all the people at the meeting agreed that they should pray for Sameha. "As I led in prayer," Marian wrote, "I knew that you would pass."

The night before the final exams Sameha passed out the chocolates and hung the new dress she had picked up at the dressmaker's in her closet. She felt different. She was no longer finding it such a struggle to keep her eyes on Jesus and his promises of help. For the first time she was not afraid.

The next day while the tests were going on I tried not to worry, but it was difficult. I kept thinking about the chocolates and the graduation dress hanging in Sameha's closet, and it was all I could do to keep from crying.

Madeline had promised to come and tell me the results as soon as they were known. The tests were to be graded immediately while the students waited, and then they were to go on to the practical test on the ward.

"You can't imagine how close it was," Madeline said. "She had seventy-nine and one-half points. The supervisor from the government was there all the time, which made everyone more nervous. The paper was so close they went over it one more time, and the second time the supervisor found they had overlooked one section that gave her the extra half point. Sameha and the rest of the students were so excited they could hardly contain themselves.

Later, when Alice was told that Sameha had passed she took the news quite calmly. She wasn't surprised. She had expected as much all along.

The graduation was beautiful. Sameha wore her new uniform and cap and stood in the courtyard in front of the chapel holding her diploma to have her picture taken. There is something special about the picture. Sameha has almost a glow of success radiating from her face. "I'm going as a nurse to Yemen," she told me later. "I'm a little bit frightened going so far from home, but I know that is where I am supposed to be."

The final arrangements had been made for us to spend our furlough year in Richmond. We packed our suitcases, stored some of our things, and left the rest so the house could be used while we were gone. As we came down to the last days, we spent a lot of our time at teas or dinners in the houses of our friends or sitting with others in the small parlor. So many things we had taken for granted had been suddenly snatched away that now we assumed nothing. "We will be back," we assured each one and yet we seemed to know that nothing was sure anymore.

My eyes lingered lovingly on each familiar scene within the hospital compound that had been our home. Then I looked up and over the wall at the minarets, domes, shops, stalls, and dusty streets of Gaza, all leading to the sea. No oranges would ever taste better than those grown in Gaza's sunny soil. No friends would ever be truer than those we had made in this far, foreign country.

I couldn't have imagined it at the time, but it would be years before I was to see this much-loved place again. I would see Alice under very different circumstances, but once again the encounter would lead to a life-changing chain of events.

We did go to Richmond, and after much work David passed his orals in surgery.

CHAPTER
17

The window was open, and a fresh breeze was blowing from the sea. The moon was hidden for a moment behind clouds, and the air was tart with the odor of lemons and *rihan*. A rooster crowed, and then there was the soft crunching sound of a car going by on the main street. It took a few minutes to realize I was in a small bedroom at Ed and Anne Nicholas's house. I was in Gaza.

The cock crowed again and was answered by another cock some distance away. I got out of bed and went to the window just as the muezzin began his mystical, lonesome call to prayer from a nearby minaret.

The return to Gaza had been exciting. It had been more than seven years since I had left. There were many changes. I had been shocked at the sign that greeted tourists as they entered Gaza, "Enter Gaza at Your Own Risk." I had missed familiar faces that were now scattered over the world in places like Canada, Australia, Brazil, and the United States. It made seeing the friends who were left all the more special.

Alice was still in Gaza. It had taken her a whole day to catch me up on all the amazing and wonderful things that had happened after I left. It made me regret that we never had written. "But what about you?" I finally asked. "Where are you living?"

Just as in the past she seemed reluctant to answer and I knew things had not gone well. "I still have a little place I am renting, but just before you came it was almost sold."

"What would you have done then?"

"I don't know. It is not easy to find someplace to rent. Everything is full and so expensive now."

"Is your little house still in danger of being sold?"

"I hope not. That was the worst thing that ever happened to me. I was put out on the street with no place to go."

"On the street? What do you mean?"

"Well, the owner had sold the house and I couldn't find anyplace to go. The day finally came when the man from Jerusalem was coming to sign the papers and pay the money. That morning while I was teaching school, the woman who owned the house moved everything I owned out into the street and that is where I found my things when I came home."

I was shocked. "What happened? What did you do?"

"The man was already here. In fact, they were sitting under a tree in my chairs drawing up the terms. I didn't know what to do. I was really frightened. I sat down on the steps and said, 'Lord, I'm always asking you to help other people and now here I am with this big problem. You haven't helped me at all. You even let them move my furniture out into the street. Can't you do something? Here I am your child and I have no place to go.' "

"Did you find another place?"

"No. There wasn't any other place. I had looked everywhere. You know Melia had died, and I had no one to help me."

"What did you do?"

"Well, my landlady said since the papers weren't signed and the man would not be back with the money until the next day I could spend the night there, but that was all."

"You left your things out all night?"

"Yes. There was nothing else to do. The next day I went to school not knowing where I would spend the next night. When I came home from school the next night the woman was at the door to meet me. She had a puzzled look on her face, and I could tell something was wrong."

"You don't have to move," she said, "I just got word that the man who was going to buy this little house was not able to after all."

"Do you know why?"

"No."

"So you are still in the same house?"

"Yes," she said, "I had to hire someone to help me get my things back inside, and I've been there ever since. She hasn't found anyone else who will pay her the price she is asking."

"But if she gets the right price you will have to move?"

"Yes, of course."

That had left me concerned about Alice. I could see that her living situation was very precarious. I regretted that I would be leaving for Jerusalem so soon and couldn't ask her more questions. There was no time. I was expected at Bob and Margaret Lindsey's house in Jerusalem the next afternoon.

It was always a treat to stay with the Lindseys. Bob had come to Israel as a student and had returned later with his wife Margaret to stay. Bob had done many things during the years he spent in Israel, but now his main expertise was the Hebrew language and some new discoveries he had made about the New Testament. He was also the pastor of the Narkis Street Baptist Church of Jerusalem. Margaret had been busy as a pastor's wife and raising their six children.

Now most of their children were married and living in the United States. "You will be staying in Debbie's room," Margaret told me.

I had last seen Debbie just after the 1967 war when our children were in the boarding school in Tel Aviv. She had been in the sixth grade, and I had remembered her as being both cute and precocious.

"There is your towel and washcloth," Margaret said. "Do you need anything else?"

"I didn't answer because I had suddenly seen on the chest of drawers a picture of the most beautiful girl I had ever seen. "Is this Debbie?" I asked picking the picture up to get a better look."

"Yes, she's changed a lot since you last saw her."

We both laughed, and I put the picture back on the chest. "I guess she's married by now isn't she?"

"No, she isn't married. She's been engaged often enough, but each time it just hasn't worked out. She even has her wedding dress, but it's never been worn."

"Well, it isn't because she isn't beautiful," I quipped.

"I keep praying for the right man to come along, but so far it hasn't happened."

We didn't talk anymore about our children, but that night I told them about Alice. "I'm writing up some of the amazing things that happened while I was in Gaza. Do you think it would be possible to find the house in Jerusalem where Alice lived as a little girl?"

"Better than finding the house would be to have Alice herself take you around to the places she remembers," Bob suggested. I was delighted. Soon the plans were made and Alice was called.

Bob had agreed to drive us. As soon as Alice arrived at the Lindsey's front door, we set out to find the house. As we passed familiar streets and buildings Alice grew more and more excited.

"There is Miss Radford's house." she said pointing to a large, impressive, stone house with a wide front porch. "I used to go there in the afternoon for Sunday School," Alice said.

"Miss Radford was known in Jerusalem for her hospitality." Bob interjected. "When I first came to Jerusalem, I went there quite often for singing and Bible study."

"Once when I was sick," Alice remembered, "she took me home and put me in bed with lots of pillows and fed me soup until I was better."

"She was a wonderful woman." Bob said as he slowly drove past the house so we could get a better look.

"When she came to visit us and my mother served her tea, she never seemed to drink all of it," Alice said. "I remember because I used to take her cup to the kitchen and drink the rest as though I were a very fine lady."

We weren't far from the Damascus Gate when Bob announced. "This is what used to be the old Arab quarter. Can you see anything that looks like your house?" He drove slowly past the large stone houses that peered over the high walls that came right out to the sidewalk.

"There, over there. That's the house." Alice was so excited she could hardly wait to get out of the car. "Do you think they would mind if we just went inside the door? Just to remember how it was?"

"No. In fact, I think they would be interested to know who lived here before they came." Bob was leading Alice up to the door.

"These people will be Israelis, Bob," I said. "You'll have to talk to them and explain. See if they will also let us look at the garden where Alice saw the vision." If I was ever going to write Alice's story, I felt I needed to see just how it looked.

Alice was the one who knocked on the door and hesitantly explained in Arabic that she had lived here with her mother and father and would like to see the house again, if it was possible. The woman called her husband. It was evident she didn't know much Arabic. When the husband came, Bob explained in Hebrew. As he talked, the man and his wife began to smile and nod, and I knew it was going to be all right.

We went inside and stood in the parlor and Alice showed us where the tree had been and where the large Bible always lay. "Now I want to take you outside and show you where I saw Jesus."

The husband understood just enough to be curious. "What does she mean she 'saw Jesus'?" he asked Bob.

"It was while she lived here that she had a vision. Jesus appeared to her and told her to warn people of the trouble that was coming. Of course there was no trouble then and most people didn't believe there would be any."

The man told his wife and both were eager to see where Alice had seen the vision. We went back out the door and around the house to the side. "Here, this is the place," Alice said. She pointed to the low, basement-like window that opened at ground level. "That is where I saw the Bible and over here is where Jesus was standing." She was eagerly pointing out the various places and didn't even notice that a crowd was gathering.

"What's this all about?" a young boy asked and then others began asking questions all at once. Bob motioned for them to be quiet while he explained. When he had finished there was a hushed silence. Finally one old man spoke up, "That is strange. It was in that same basement room that some old rabbis used to gather to copy the Torah. It is a holy place."

Now more people arrived and joined the crowd to find out what was happening. Each time Alice would tell her story and Bob would interpret. Finally, it became evident that we would have to leave or we would never get anything else done.

We got back into the car and waved to the small crowd that had gathered. They had wished me well on writing the book, and I wished I could have spoken without needing an interpreter.

Bob let us out at the Joppa Gate. I wanted to see the Church of the Holy Sepulchre as Alice had seen it when she went there with her father. I was not disappointed. Every area had some memory. "See this big urn with that brown, woodlike rock in it," Alice said, "They always told us that was Adam's skull. Look, see how that woman is kissing the nail print on Jesus' hand in the picture. We always used to do that too."

We climbed the steep stairs that led to the section of the church that was believed to have been the hill of Calvary. Now it resembled a very ornate balcony. On the far side was a hole outlined in silver where the cross was supposed to have stood. Immediately over the hole was a table, and around it were pictures and candelabra of all kinds. "We used to crawl under that table to kiss the spot where the cross stood and as a little girl I would then look up to the ceiling where there is a picture of Jesus looking down at us. That was the part I loved most of all."

As we came out of the church Alice pointed to a large door off to the right. "My father always stopped in the chapel of Saint James. It would have been here that his body was brought for the funeral after he died." We went in and saw where he would have worshiped, and then Alice asked if we could go to the Greek cemetery where he was buried.

This was perhaps the saddest part of the whole venture. Though we walked up and down reading hundreds of markers we could never find the tomb of her father. "I remember it well. We used to come here, all of us—Mother, Melia, George, and I," Alice said.

It was getting late when we finally met Bob again at the Joppa Gate. We were exhausted. We had walked from one end of the market to the other and had examined carefully every interesting spot in the Church of the Holy Sepulchre.

"I'm going to take you back to the house," Bob said, "so Alice can get a warm bit of tea before she starts back to Gaza."

The tea was just what we needed, and the sandwiches Margaret made were gone in no time. We looked at the clock. It was almost time for Alice to go if she were going to catch her taxi.

"Alice, I have just thought of something. Without the thoughtfulness of Bob and Margaret this day would never have happened. I wonder if there isn't something they need that we could pray about before you leave."

"Yes," Alice said, "That is a good idea. What would you like us to pray about?"

"I can't think of anything we really need," Bob said.

"We don't *need* anything," Margaret said, "but there is something I want for my children. Danny and his wife have tried for three years to have a child. They want one desperately. Could you pray for them, Alice?"

"Of course, I will be glad to pray and see what the answer is."

Then Margaret said, "There is my daughter Debbie. She is so pretty and she has been engaged a number of times, but it has never been quite right. Will you pray for her?"

We stood in a circle and Alice prayed a very simple, direct prayer, and then it was time for her to go. As she was leaving she stopped and looked at Bob and Margaret, "Don't worry about your son or your daughter. Your prayers will be answered."

After that special day with Alice in Jerusalem the time really flew, and before I knew it I was on the plane headed for home. Months later I met some friends who said, "Have you heard about the Lindsey's grandchildren? Their son and his wife had triplets. One of them died, but the other two are just fine."

"Which son had the triplets?" I asked eagerly.

"It was Danny. They had wanted children for such a long time and now triplets."

The conversation quickly changed, but I remembered the prayer and right away thought of their daughter, Debbie. I wondered what, if anything, had happened to her.

How surprised I would have been at that time to know that within a few years Debbie would be marrying one of my sons. They hadn't seen each other since the fifth grade. Both had shared similar experiences but at different times and in different places. Often Debbie had just left as John arrived or vice versa. However, they had mutual friends, and John seemed to be constantly hearing about her.

Finally, as John himself tells it, he felt definitely impressed to pray for Debbie every day. Gradually, as he prayed for her, he began to feel that she was to play some important role in his life even to the point of becoming his wife. This was so strange that he told no one but like Mary, "pondered it in his heart."

He began to write to Debbie and then sent her some tapes when he was in the country of Yemen on a relief project. He hinted that when his tour of duty was over, he might come to Tulsa to see her on his way to California to visit his brother.

When they finally met in Tulsa, it took only one day for them to realize that they were in love and wanted to be engaged.

When we all got together for the wedding three months later, we remembered Alice and the wonderful day in Jerusalem. "Do you think it is possible that without Alice's prayer this would ever have happened?" I asked. No one answered. We just thought about it and then I said, "Well, if Alice were here she would say asking is important, and Margaret asked. Faith is important, and Alice certainly has faith. It reminds me of Jesus' words, 'Ask and it shall be given you; seek, and ye shall find; knock, and it shall be opened unto you.'"

As closely as I have examined and questioned Alice there is very little that I can prove to the average skeptic, but I know what it has done for me. I have realized that we have only tapped a thimbleful of what Jesus wants to do for us and in us.

There is much more that could be written, but I have chosen to write only of those things I actually saw or was on the spot to investigate. There is nothing wrong with, "[examining] the spirits" (1 John 4:1). We are told to do that in the Bible. Not every miraculous happening is of God, and in our day especially we need to learn the difference.

As I watched Alice, some things were very evident. She prayed in Jesus' name and gave him all the credit for what was done. Just like Jesus, when he prayed for people, Alice prayed because she wanted to help people. She never accepted money and instead of being thanked she was often made fun of and criticized.

Perhaps most interesting is the way she prays to find God's will in a matter and then acts on the answer. Most of us have had a similar experience, but it has taken weeks or months to find God's will. "Thy will be done in earth, as it is in heaven" Jesus prayed. For Alice that is the very essence of prayer—to find God's will.